ACPL ITEM
DISCARDE

D0905833

658 W52q
Westland, Cynthia Lane, 1953
-
Quality

Quality:

The I

DO NOT REMOVE
CARDS FROM POCKET

ALLEN COUNTY PUBLIC LIBRARY

FORT WAYNE, INDIANA 46802

You may return this book to any agency, branch,
or bookmobile of the Allen County Public Library.

DEMCO

Quality:
The Myth and The Magic

CYNTHIA LANE WESTLAND

 ASQC Quality Press
Milwaukee, Wisconsin

Allen County Public Library
Ft. Wayne, Indiana

QUALITY: THE MYTH AND THE MAGIC
CYNTHIA LANE WESTLAND

Library of Congress Cataloging-in-Publication Data

Westland, Cynthia Lane.
    Quality: the myth and the magic / Cynthia Lane Westland.
      p.   cm.
    Includes bibliographical references and index.
    ISBN 0-87389-088-4
    1. Organizational effectiveness. 2. Organizational change.
    3. Quality of products. I. Title
    HD58.9.W47 1990   90-37351
    658—dc20   CIP

Copyright© 1990 by ASQC Quality Press
All rights reserved. No part of this book may be reproduced in any form or by any means, electronic, mechanical, photocopying, recording, or otherwise, without the prior permission of the publisher.

10 9 8 7 6 5 4 3 2 1

ISBN   0-87389-088-4

Acquisitions Editor: Jeanine L. Lau
Production Editor: Tammy Griffin
Cover design by Wayne Dober.
Set in Bookman by DanTon Typographers. Printed and bound by BookCrafters.

PRINTED IN THE UNITED STATES OF AMERICA

 ASQC Quality Press
310 West Wisconsin Avenue
Milwaukee, Wisconsin 53203

This book is dedicated with love to the memory of my father, Robert Edson Lane, for giving me a sense of wonder and making me believe that all my childhood dreams could come true, and to my mother, Mary Eleanor, for providing a framework in which to make them real.

Contents

Preface

We stand at the fork in the road between success and failure in the marketplace.

The roles we now play as contributors to and leaders of American corporations will determine the economic destiny of our future and our children's futures.

We have the power and the means to secure the competitive edge necessary for achieving the kind of spectacular results that Edison, Ford, Franklin, and Bell achieved in their lifetimes if we use the same type of thinking and never say never. We are a product of a legacy of risk takers, pioneers, and inventors. In meeting the challenges of the (new frontier) marketplace it is worth remembering the actions of some of the people who shaped our history. This book is about risk and payoff. It is about finding the right mix of technical expertise and human systems (personal touch) required to deliver excellence in the marketplace.

This book is about heroes and heroines; it is about shattering the myths that keep us from achieving the greatness inside each of us and replacing them with the magic that comes from challenges met and exceeded. It is about empowerment, dedication, commitment, and American ingenuity.

In writing this book, I have put aside the notion that "Made in America" carries some tarnished connotation and that the Japanese strategy is the answer.

I hope you will find it stimulating and thought provoking.

Cynthia Lane Westland

Quality:

The Myth and The Magic

CHAPTER 1

Introduction

The process of achieving world class quality status involves a rigorous, aggressive, and total commitment to superior quality in all things. It is a well-planned, well-executed, and sharply focused doctrine. It is a commitment of minds, hearts, and resources that transcends slogans and edicts. It is not for the timid, the weak, or the rigid, for its success comes from the courage to act, the strength to endure, and the flexibility to change.

The first mistake we make as senior managers is in the way we envision our organization. We tend to view the organization as an "it" and "us" association, in which "it" (the organization) is an autonomous entity, separate and distinct from the "us" who are affected by "it." This is analogous to thinking of our physical bodies as independent of the components that make them up.

From a total quality improvement standpoint, when we merely treat a symptom (i.e., problem) in the organization we may gain some short-term improvement through emergency treatment— the quick fix which results in the alleviation of the pain for the moment. In the long run, the patient—the organization—may die of an underlying, more serious root-cause disease.

It is, therefore, logical to assume that if people make up organizations, and the organization exists to service its customers (i.e., more people), then we should build and promote the superior emotional, moral, and intellectual characteristics which set the outstanding apart from the mediocre.

PRESCRIPTION FOR CORPORATE WELLNESS
WORLD CLASS STATUS

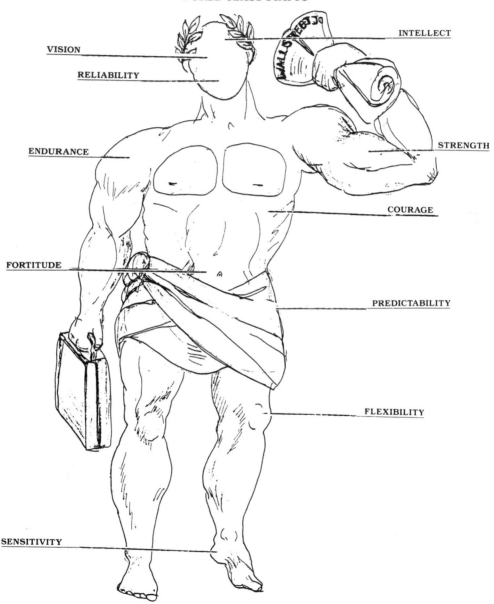

If we were to examine superior people who operate in a state of "wellness," we would probably see the following human traits:

1. *Strength.*   The ability to exercise force, power, and vigor, and to resist attack.

2. *Endurance.*   The ability to withstand pain, distress, and fatigue, and to sustain oneself.

3. *Flexibility.*   The ability to "bend without breaking," to change, and to modify or be influenced by new ideas and methods.

4. *Reliability.*   The ability to be trustworthy and relied on in all types of situations; personal credibility.

5. *Predictability.*   Behavior that is stable with no radical changes in nature.

6. *Sensitivity.*   The awareness of and response to the needs of others.

7. *Intellect.*   The outstanding capability to reason, understand, and analyze information.

8. *Responsibility.*   The accountability for one's own behavior and the demonstration of superior dependability, trustworthiness, and reliability.

9. *Innovation.*   The dissatisfaction with things the way they are; the search for new methods, technologies, and improvements as a part of personal satisfaction.

Similarly, there are outstanding corporations which possess these same characteristics. Companies of strength are financially and technologically capable of exerting power and dominance in the marketplace.

- *Companies of endurance* are guided by a strategic plan that allows them to maintain the necessary competitive advantage to survive during recessions, market shifts, offshore competition, and materials cost escalation.

- *Flexible companies* are the ones that can change or modify their existing products and/or services to meet changing customer demands on a timely basis.

- *Reliable companies* are those that have been able to make a "name" for themselves from a quality and/or service standpoint.

These are companies whose products and services meet customer requirements consistently without failure.

- *Predictable companies* are those whose past superior performance is the basis for the expected quality of future products and services.

- *Sensitive companies* are aware of, and make use of, the needs and desires of their customers. They have a full customer satisfaction thrust in all facets of business practice.

- *Intelligent companies* listen to the needs and requirements of their customers, both the positive and the negative. They process the information, analyze the technology and human systems issues, and consistently make good business decisions.

- *Responsible companies* are leaders in the area of accountability in all of their business practices.

- *Innovative companies* are not content to go on with "business as usual," but are engaged in developing new ways to service their customers through the exploration of new ideas and new technologies.

This book discusses the managerial, structural, and technological changes necessary to set the stage for the quality improvement process. Additionally, it details how to implement the necessary systems to optimize successful change and become *world class* in products and services.

Contrary to other approaches based on Japanese methodology, I believe that not only can American business excel, but it can dominate the marketplace by capitalizing on our native cultural assets of individualism, innovation, and healthy competition. The approach to achieving true customer satisfaction and superior quality presented in this book is designed for U.S. companies and is driven by our unique cultural heritage as Americans.

I hope that this book will be a valuable asset to American business in understanding the contribution of quality professionals in organizations and applying the technical and managerial skills necessary to achieve world class quality and complete customer satisfaction.

CHAPTER 2

Barriers to Improvement

● We're Different—It Won't Work Here

The first barrier to improvement is the idea of "uniqueness." The "we're different — it won't work here" mentality is responsible for many quality improvement processes never getting off the ground. Some other typical responses used as excuses for not getting started go something like this:

- *We make a unique product.*
- *We provide a unique service.*
- *We have a different/new technology.*
- *We are:*
    a. *too small; or*
    b. *too large; or*
    c. *a start-up company, so that doesn't fit our situation.*

- *We don't have:*
  - **a.** *enough time; or*
  - **b.** *enough money; or*
  - **c.** *enough resources, etc.*

Largely, these responses are caused by the lack of understanding by senior and middle management of quality improvement and its direct link to profit, market share, and superior customer service. The burden of education in the quality improvement process has in the past rested with the quality professional. In the future, it will be essential that management understand the role of quality in meeting the needs of internal and external customers to secure a competitive position in the marketplace and to maximize profit. This role is the same, regardless of the "uniqueness" of a particular industry or company.

It is helpful to note that the use of fundamental skills of quality engineering in quality measurement, strategic planning evaluation, and improvement are similar to the application of techniques in the engineering, marketing, sales, and finance disciplines. For example, the basic work methods and procedures used by financial professionals in developing a Profit and Loss (P&L) statement are the same, regardless of whether the corporation is a financial institution, a high technology manufacturing company, or a family-owned "mom and pop" store. While variations of the specific information required on the P&L statement will be made by the preparer, the techniques, skills, and execution of the basic P&L statement will be the same.

The same principle of successfully applying quality engineering skills, techniques, and methods to different service and manufacturing companies holds true. An example of this can be seen in the preparation of a *quality cost diagnostic*, a tool used to determine the cost of non-value-added activities in an organization. When preparing the quality cost diagnostic, the process of interviewing, data collection, evaluation, and validation is identical, regardless of the type of organization being evaluated. The variation occurs in the finished product (the diagnostic document) with regard to the specific line items as they may be unique to a particular company or industry. Further, the use of other quality engineering techniques for process capability, statistical process control, failure analysis, trend analysis, value analysis, and problem solving proves the rule of organization "uniqueness" by virtue of size, industry, technology, or culture. It is not a deterrent to the institution of a successful quality improvement process.

● I'm OK, You're Not

The second barrier to quality improvement is the belief that quality is the other guy's responsibility, and that bad quality, product, or service is someone else's fault. This is known as the "I'm OK, you're not" syndrome. Until there is ownership of an organization's problems by all of its members, and finger pointing and condemnation ceases, no sustaining improvement can take place.

Eliminating the "I'm OK, you're not" syndrome and achieving total involvement of all employees begins with senior management commitment.

● Product Excellence and Doublespeak

Commitment of senior management involves the daily practice of internal and external customer satisfaction and quality-first principles. It is sustained through a quality-by-example versus a quality-by-exception work ethic. The extent to which management embraces and practices quality for full customer satisfaction is critical to the success of the quality improvement process.

The "litmus test" of commitment can be seen when managers are faced with the prospect of no ship, line shutdown, and product recall situations. In the resolution of nonconforming materials and products and out-of-control processes, consideration for customer satisfaction must be the deciding factor.

Verbal commitment to product excellence must be reinforced by quality in practice. There must be consistency in the standards by which a product, process, or service is achieved and accepted. Only in this way, can the commitment remain real, the focus of the company remain strong, and the improvement process maintain credibility.

It is therefore a management responsibility to drive quality improvement, not by convenience, but by a decision-making process anchored in providing superior customer service and increased customer satisfaction.

● Telephone—The Childhood Game Played in Adult Corporate America

Communication is a critical issue in achieving product, process, and service quality. If communication is poor, it can be a barrier to the improvement process.

Many of us are familiar with a childhood game called "telephone." The objective of the game is to communicate a piece of information by whispering in the ear of the person next to you and letting that person continue the process until all of the players receive the information. The last person to receive the information then announces to the group what he or she heard.

Invariably, the exercise proved that what was announced at the end of the process bore little similarity to what was said by the originator of the information. In corporate America, this game is played constantly. As information comes from the top of the organization down to middle management and on down to the worker, it often becomes obscured to the point that it creates confusion, anxiety, and misinterpretation.

Lack of clear communication is a serious impediment to the improvement process. Much of the success of the improvement process stems from complete understanding of the corporate vision (i.e., a concise set of objectives formulated to support the overall direction of the company), and the translation of that vision into corporate goals.

Typically, the reaction to inadequate or inaccurate communication results in the following:

- Blurring of the corporate vision.
- Misinterpretation of information.
- The tendency to do anything to show responsiveness.

The overwhelming desire to respond in a timely manner overshadows the need to validate the information with the originator; consequently, internal customer service breaks down.

The remedy for top-down communication problems involves the ability of senior management to create and foster an environment of trust, and daily interaction with middle management and workers.

● The Trust Factor—Getting Rid of Fear of the Unknown

Many of the stumbling blocks that occur in business between top management and the rest of the work force are the result of senior management not knowing its immediate customers' (the work force) wants and needs. The same holds true of the work force in regard to senior management. One of the best cures for this problem from a management standpoint is *visibility*. It is important that the top management of a corporation take the time to be personally involved in the communication process between themselves and their people in a way that is more than stating they have an open door policy. Management commitment takes place only when management actually open the door; commitment is improved when they step outside the door and periodically reacquaint themselves with the work force, the process, and the end product or service.

In this way, two things of value occur: (1) management get first-hand knowledge of how things are going; and (2) management reinforce the verbal commitment to open communication downward through the organization. By this type of action, management will build the kind of trust which fosters better understanding of the situations faced by the work force daily. It will also enable management to better service their primary internal customer.

But what about the external customer? Part of the efforts of managers to understand the needs of their external customers requires the resolution of customer complaints. This process may take many forms, including the following:

- Direct customer contact.
- Survey of customers.
- Review of written complaints.
- Involvement in field problems as part of a troubleshooting team.

- Following the customer dissatisfaction route from its first appearance to its final resolution.

By engaging in the customer dissatisfaction journey, we can see how the internal errors of the organization directly and indirectly contribute to the loss of good will, loss of repeat business, and eventual loss of market share.

To illustrate this point, let's consider what happens from both the customer standpoint and the supplier standpoint when superior customer service is not the driving focus of the organization.

WHAT HAPPENED AS THE CUSTOMER SEES IT	WHAT HAPPENED AS THE SUPPLIER SEES IT
• Product received on due date, but damaged—will not operate in selected modes. • Customer dissatisfied.	• Product shipped on time fit for use to the customer. • Supplier satisfied with meeting schedule.

The following represents a typical scenario arising from the receipt of rejected product from the supplier at the customer's facility. The first reconstruction shows the short-term and long-term results.

CUSTOMER	SUPPLIER
• Customer complaint generated. Request for return of product.	• Customer complaint noted. Return request authorized.
• Customer packages product to supplier with letter stating reasons for return.	• Supplier receives return product in shop.
• Customer awaits resolution of problem.	• Supplier examines returned product and customer documentation. • Supplier retests product. • Supplier repairs product. • Supplier inspects product. • Product is packaged for shipment back to the customer.
• Customer waits for 12 days.	• Corrected product is shipped back to the customer.
• Customer receives "fixed" product.	

On the surface, it would seem that this was a story with a small conflict which was corrected and resulted in a happy ending. That is exactly what is wrong with "doing business as usual." If we examine that same story more closely, we will see that:

1. The conflict was more than minor.
2. The correction was costly to both supplier and customer.
3. The problem has not truly been resolved.

Many managers working in the crisis or "firefighting" mode would have handled the problem in a similar fashion. Standard operating procedure is to fix the problem of the day and then move on to the next problem of the day. When this management technique is used, it results in a temporary, short-term fix rather than a long-term resolution. Was the repair of the customer's product providing superior customer service? No. Was it providing some satisfaction? Temporarily, for the short term. Let's look at what happened to that same customer *one month later*. . . .

WHAT HAPPENED AS THE CUSTOMER SAW IT	WHAT HAPPENED AS THE SUPPLIER SAW IT
• Product received on due date, but damaged. • Product will not operate in selected modes. • Customer dissatisfied. Must return product for repair for the second time in thirty days. Impact to customer in meeting their commitments.	• Product shipped on time fit for use to the customer. • Supplier satisfied with meeting schedule.

Now the supplier is faced with dealing with customer dissatisfaction at an escalated level. Typically, when customers are dealing with chronic quality problems, the level of the organization at which the supplier is contacted is elevated from the customer service department to the quality director or sometimes to the president of the company. It is usually at this "customer big noise" level that serious efforts are undertaken to alleviate the problem and institute a long-term solution. The hope is that the supplier has not lost future business and can recoup the good will of the customer.

In any case, the goal of superior customer service and world class quality has not been met by the supplier. When we examine the customer satisfaction chain of events more closely, we see that the company vision of superior customer satisfaction has become secondary to:

• Making the build/ship schedule.

• Fixing errors for short-term gain.

- Maintaining a reactionary posture versus quality planning based on present customer needs and in anticipation of future customer needs.

To more completely understand all of the ramifications of the customer dissatisfaction story, it is necessary to quantify all of the activities expended in an effort to make bad product or service good. The ability to put non-value-added activities into financial language will enable people at all levels of the organization to understand the adverse company-wide impact of errors and waste.

● Quality Costs—A Window into the Improvement Process

An essential element in the process of determining corporate quality health is the *quality cost analysis*. The purpose of the quality cost analysis is to quantify all of the non-value-added waste activities of the organization and to identify the greatest opportunities for improvement. It also provides a mechanism for the following:

- Monitoring of the cost reduction realized through the improvement process.
- Evaluation of the effectiveness of corrective action programs.
- Allocation of resources against those items isolated for improvement.

The traditional way of categorizing quality costs follows.

1. *Prevention costs.*   Measures taken to preclude future errors. Examples: training, equipment calibration, preventative maintenance programs, process capability studies.

2. *Appraisal costs.*   Activities involving the detection of errors. Examples: invoice reviews, test, inspection, engineering change order activity.

3. *Internal costs.*   Activities performed to correct errors that are identified in the appraisal process *prior* to the delivery of the product or service to the customer. Examples: scrap, rework, payroll error, equipment downtime.

4. *External costs.* Activities performed to correct errors identified *after* the delivery of the product or service to the customer. Examples: field repair, customer returns, product liability suits, failure reports, returned material reports.

When collecting cost of quality information we want to focus on corporate waste, that is, all activities which add no value to the end product or service and those which have direct/indirect market damage. As we begin to address the questions of corporate waste we can think of the contributing factors in this way:

- Waste of *materials.*
- Waste of *time.*
- Waste of *resources.*
- Waste of *equipment.*

As we examine the specific waste categories, it is helpful to further classify them:

- Cost of *management error.*
- Cost of *worker error.*
- Cost of *supplier error.*
- Cost of *equipment error.*

By expanding the non-valued-added activities of the organization to include all three sets of criteria, an *evaluation matrix* can be set up concurrent with the cost data for each discrete line item. The sample evaluation matrix illustrates the use of the three sets of criteria in establishing quality financial data and attributing an error category and identifying a corresponding waste category.

QUALITY COST EVALUATION MATRIX

ITEM	COST CATEGORY				ERROR CATEGORY				WASTE CATEGORY				$ RESULT
	Prevention	Appraisal	Internal	External	Management Error	Worker Error	Supplier Error	(Proc) Equipment Error	Waste of Materials	Waste of Time	Waste of Resources	Waste of Equipment	Cost (Thousands)
Scrap			X					X	X	X	X	X	100
Rework			X				X			X	X	X	65
R.T.V.			X				X		X	X	X		40
Inspection		X				X				X	X		410
Test		X								X	X	X	350
Equipment calibration	X												20
Product recall				X					X	X	X	X	250
Training	X			X									30
M.R.B.		X								X	X		25
Missed delivery				X	X					X	X		70
Short shipments				X	X					X	X		50
Billing errors		X			X					X	X		15
R&D	X												225
Equipment downtime			X			X				X	X	X	80
Obsolete material		X			X				X	X	X	X	190
Excess inventory	X				X				X	X	X	X	1,200

Quality Cost Assessment versus Quality Cost Diagnostic

Before the corporation can reach the level of detail necessary to identify the cause of a high quality cost item, a quality cost assessment and a quality cost diagnostic should be performed.

The first phase of the quality cost assessment is accomplished by defining the quality cost and educating management in its uses. The assessment process can be accomplished in any of the following four ways:

1. An internal quality expert educates top management to enable them to teach middle management, with middle managers actually performing the assessment.

2. An internal quality professional works with senior management to lead the assessment/evaluation.

3. An outside consultant with substantial experience in cost of quality analysis leads the assessment in the role of educator to senior and middle management.

4. An outside consultant performs the assessment.

The second phase of the quality assessment defines the work to be performed and the data required. A review of the existing cost data is conducted and interview questions are developed to ascertain some estimates which will aid in forming the baseline cost data.

Next, the interview process is conducted and work-in-process is observed. The information is organized and the data arrayed according to the quality cost categories. The baseline measurement data are established and used to identify the high cost, quality improvement areas of opportunity.

In the final phase, a preliminary analysis of the data is made considering cost, waste category, and error category. Recommendations for quality improvement can be made based on the supporting documentation. The quality cost flow chart on the following page depicts the phases of the assessment process.

The outcome of the assessment will be the foundation upon which the diagnostic information can be built into the quality planning and improvement process.

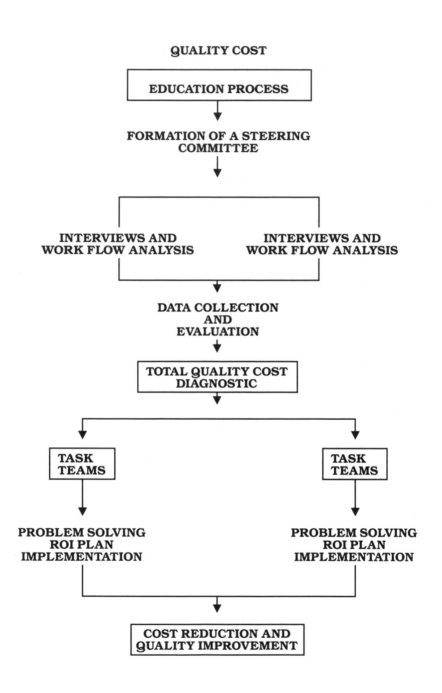

QUALITY COST

EDUCATION PROCESS

FORMATION OF A STEERING
COMMITTEE

INTERVIEWS AND
WORK FLOW ANALYSIS

INTERVIEWS AND
WORK FLOW ANALYSIS

DATA COLLECTION
AND
EVALUATION

TOTAL QUALITY COST
DIAGNOSTIC

TASK
TEAMS

TASK
TEAMS

PROBLEM SOLVING
ROI PLAN
IMPLEMENTATION

PROBLEM SOLVING
ROI PLAN
IMPLEMENTATION

COST REDUCTION AND
QUALITY IMPROVEMENT

Service Industry Quality Cost Assessment. A quality cost analysis would not be complete without a discussion of the methods used in determining the cost of service industry quality.

Cycle time and customer satisfaction data are two significant components in determining the level of service quality and associated cost. Internal cycle time for such items as forms, internal reports, and response times for data input or feedback are used to determine cost. In a health care setting, for example, one method of determining quality costs would be to measure the cycle time taken to have a patient admitted to the hospital. The total cycle time for filling out paperwork, giving medical history, preliminary admittance testing, and final room assignment can be measured and costed. Additionally, the cost of errors associated with the process would be identified and costed as waste. Incorrect or incomplete paperwork, transposition errors, and patient retesting are examples of service quality costs in a health care setting.

Evaluation of surgical quality procedures would include the number of successful operations performed in all categories (i.e., critical, major, and minor), number of operations performed without complications, etc. Patient or customer satisfaction would be measured by things such as degree of comfort and lack of pain experienced by the patient; response time by medical staff to patient's needs; accuracy of diagnostic evaluation; and patient feedback from the doctor regarding test results, diagnosis, prognosis, and available options. Patient or customer dissatisfaction cost categories would include such things as retesting due to staff or equipment error, incorrect diagnosis, slow response time to patient needs, surgical complications resulting from physician error (malpractice), and billing errors (double billing/incorrect billing) for hospital or out-patient care.

To achieve the level of information necessary to begin the improvement process (implementation), it is necessary to execute a quality cost diagnostic. The diagnostic is a micro-level identification of non-valued-added activities for which specific action can be taken to realize improvement. Additionally, the diagnostic serves as a measure of the corrective action taken.

First, a steering committee is formed to oversee and administrate the project teams engaged in the improvement process. The committee prioritizes the projects and begins to establish the quality business plan. A more detailed data collection takes place, primarily to break down the assessment cost figures into smaller numbers which can be used by the task teams. The new data are then evaluated and validated.

Finally, an implementation strategy is solidified, task teams are established, and problem-solving techniques are taught. At this point, the teams are armed with enough information and tools to initiate the resolution of chronic, high cost problems and to begin the continuous improvement process. The flow chart illustrates the process (see page 16). As the high cost items are resolved and costs are reduced, product and service quality will increase along with customer satisfaction.

In the process of continuous improvement, the targets are to raise the level of quality for internal and external customers, reduce costs, and eliminate and/or reduce variation where possible.

Review corporate financial information to determine the following:

1. What type of cost information is presently being collected?

2. How is the information collected and consolidated?

3. Who in the organization receives the information?

Before executing the cost assessment and the cost diagnostic, managers and supervisors need to be educated in the following:

- Definition of quality cost terms.
- Quality costs in blue collar and white collar areas.
- How quality costs tie into the financial system.
- How quality costs fit into the process of total quality.
- How quality costs can be used by managers to manage their business improvement.
- How quality costs focus management attention on major improvement opportunities.
- How quality costs are used as a measurement tool in the improvement process.
- How quality costs are used to determine corporate quality wellness.
- How quality costs are integrated with other improvement programs to reduce costs and increase customer satisfaction.
- How the interview process is useful in developing estimate data and assessing overall quality awareness.

- How to use quality costs as a performance gauge.
- The use of designed experiments in determining internal cost data and identifying process improvement opportunities.

Evaluation of Cost Data.   Once the data have been gathered and arrayed, they are ready to be evaluated and analyzed. Some helpful tools in conducting the evaluation phase include the following:

1. Use of Pareto analysis to array the data. The Pareto analysis establishes cost opportunities in order of magnitude.
2. Linking the data to error and waste categories. As described in the quality cost evaluation matrix on page 14.
3. Use of a Juran product cost matrix to determine non-value-added cost by product/product line. The Juran product cost matrix measures cost by product line.
4. Benchmarking cost criteria against competitors/industry leaders (with an emphasis on customer service). This tool allows management to identify what their cost opportunities are relative to those of world class corporations.

An additional element that needs to be considered in the process is feedback. How the data are presented can be as critical as the data themselves. For this reason, the following topics should be covered when presenting the completed cost information:

- IIow to interpret the data.
- How to organize the data for improvement.
- How to measure results.
- How to tie the results to corporate goals.
- How to measure the effectiveness of the corrective action taken.
- How to evaluate customer satisfaction feedback.
- How to "work the issues" raised by the quality cost diagnostic without alienating the work force and middle managers.

The orientation of the organization in terms of how it sees quality costs is crucial in optimizing this powerful measurement/improvement tool. Some of the best efforts of companies in identifying opportunities for improvement have failed due to incorrect presentation of the data.

Cost information must be approached in a nonthreatening manner, that is, in a way that does not place blame on individuals or departments. All of the persons in the organization share equally in the responsibility to produce superior products and service consistently.

Although senior management will have overall responsibility for setting the corporate quality strategy, the improvement process should begin with managers and supervisors. People at this level of the organization, those who have *first-hand knowledge and experience*, must take responsibility and lead the implementation process within the organization. It is important to note here that when managers and workers have direct control over the identified areas of improvement, they can affect the greatest positive change in the shortest amount of time. Additionally, the "buy in" of managers and the work force through hands-on involvement adds credibility to the improvement process, lowers anxiety levels, and allows for the strongest link between understanding the concept of quality costs as an improvement tool and experiencing their own success story.

Indicators for Diagnosis

One area of major concern when trying to bring an organization to world class quality is the quality education of the organization. To assess the sophistication level of the organization requires an investigation of the people, the processes, and the end product or service from the customer point of view. Along with the formal assessment, there are also some quick indicators which will key the consultant into where, on the quality maturity grid, the organization lies. I'll call these *Dead Giveaways*.

Dead Giveaway Number One: No Recognition of Key Names and Phrases. If a client cannot tell the difference between Bing Crosby, Phil Crosby, and Crosby, Stills, Nash, and Young, we are starting from scratch in the world class quality journey. If, when asked to define repeatability, he answers that it is the ability to echo what has just been said, we are going to get to world class quality in inches, not in miles. If he identifies FMS as something that happens to his female staff, causing mood swings and other strange behavior, chances are he will never be taking that world class quality walk.

Dead Giveaway Number Two: A Physical Layout Conducive to Making No-Tech Product. If, during the course of a plant tour, I am unable to differentiate between a facility for the production of twentieth-century goods, and a brochure depicting a closeout sale of equipment from an Egyptian pyramid maker, world class quality is more than a hieroglyph away. When walking on the production floor, if the most high-tech item I can see is a neon exit sign, I usually take that as a cue and proceed quickly and quietly, as in the case of a real emergency.

If office space is so tight that you can have lunch in the cafeteria without leaving your work station, you may have just-in-time cuisine but a world class quality ulcer. When the lighting is so poor that a class in candlemaking is paid for by the company and the specifications are printed in braille, concern for employee welfare is not high on the list of priorities as part of the quality commitment. Perhaps a mushroom colony?

Dead Giveaway Number Three: A Work Force That Looks As If It Has Gone Through a Food Processor. Chances are that if blank stares, hollow eyes, and pale skin predominate the halls of this facility, there may be an epidemic in town. One that comes from overwork, confused signals, and having been led down the corporate garden path once too often. Other signs of a disturbed work force include:

- *Cyanide poisoning.* Death caused by being left out in the cold too often during sub-zero temperatures. (Also known as "singing the blues.")

- *Squamous cell carcinoma.* Death that results from third-degree burns caused by sitting in the "corporate hot seat" without sun protection.

- *Acoustic neurinoma.* Hearing loss associated with exposing the unprotected ear to high-pitched yelling by angry customers over the telephone line or directly into the ear itself. (Permanent hearing loss is experienced when the customer blows a police whistle into the phone to show displeasure regarding the mismanagement of his or her complaint.)

- *Cirrhosis of the liver.* A painful disease associated with too many cocktails while trying to swing that big deal. (Usually seen in driven members of the sales department.)

- *Hypoglycemia.* The result of verbal beatings from management shortly after a sugar high of praise. (One verbal beating negates three sugar-coated "atta' boys.") Three or more verbal beatings in one month can induce insulin shock, coma, and death.

- *Eczema.* Crusting and scaling of the skin caused by having been left out in the sun to dry by management on numerous occasions.

- *Migraine.* Severe headache, with or without associated visual and gastric disturbances, usually brought on by one of the following: (1) having all of your people call in sick on the same day; (2) getting the third special assignment of the day and being told that it is also due tomorrow; or (3) losing the receipts to your last expense account, finding them, forgetting to make a copy, and then having the accounting department lose them.

Dead Giveaway Number Four: Middle Managers Who Are Twilight Zone Contenders. It is a sure bet that if middle managers are so strange you consider calling in "ghostbusters," world class quality will be a major struggle for this organization. One classic sign of disturbed middle management includes talking *and* answering oneself. Disagreeing with oneself and having a knock-down, drag-out fight with oneself is cause for immediate confinement. Another sign is hearing voices, especially when they are the voices of animated cartoon characters or people no longer in this life. If you hear Joan of Arc, Flipper, or Hamlet, get thee to a hospital for treatment!

Other signs of something terribly wrong with the corporate picture are middle managers suffering from any of the following:

- *Vertigo.* Loss of equilibrium due to putting yourself too high on a pedestal. If a nosebleed accompanies dizziness, you are definitely sitting up too high. Apply ice packs to stop the bleeding and try removing the three issues of Yellow Pages from your chair until the dizziness passes.

- *Hydrocephalus.* Swelling of the head and resultant dementia caused by being full of oneself. Try thinking of some minor fault or omission you may have in your lifetime for which you actually took the blame. Try to think about successes that were not the result of your superior skills alone. If swelling persists, try taking a hat pin to your head.

- *Hyperactivity.* Hyperkinetic behavior caused by the fear of staying in one place long enough to be found by the CEO, your staff, or a customer. Cutting out sugar and caffeine may bring some relief. If all else fails try valium and a straightjacket.

- *Photosensitivity.* Also known as Mushroom's Disease. Occurs in managers who are afraid to come out of their offices because they may be called upon to make a decision. Some have been known to keep a complete stock of essential items such as food, beverages, and toiletries to preclude them from making an appearance during the daylight hours. Also known as Dracula's Disease.

- *Hirsutism.* Excessive hair growth usually occurring in the same cycle as the full moon. Other signs of onset are beastly behavior (howling and scratching) and an insatiable craving for hemoglobin. Cures include a silver bullet and a straight razor. Also known as Wolfman's Wisp Disease.

- *Tachycardia.* Rapid heartbeat caused by any of the following: (1) the inability to answer a key question at a senior staff meeting; (2) explaining a $500 dinner for two to the chief financial officer; (3) explaining a budget overrun of 30 percent to the controller; (4) explaining to your star performer why he or she will not be getting a promotion for the second year in a row; or (5) explaining to that same star performer why, although there was no money to reward him or her, you are getting a $25,000 company car.

Finally, this brings me to the very top of the organization where the buck should stop, but many times cannot be removed with a crow-bar from the hands of the tight-fisted bean counter. (But that is another issue!) Suffice to say that the ability of top management to understand, embrace, and act in the quality improvement process is critical to any long-term improvement and subsequent hope of becoming world class.

The higher one goes up the corporate ladder, the more likely one is to suffer from diseases of the mind rather than diseases of the body. This is why only well-adjusted bodies and minds are right for the quality improvement process. At the top of the organization, senior staff members may be plagued by phobias that affect the business lives of those in their employ. It is for this reason that I am including some Dead Giveaways which pertain mostly to the upper echelon of the corporation.

Dead Giveaway Number Five: When Anxiety Attacks Strike Get Out of the Line of Fire.   Phobias cause people to have anxiety about what they fear. The heartbeat and pulse quicken and behavior may be anything from happiness to deep depression. Whatever phobia the senior staff suffers from, one thing is sure — you don't want to be there when it happens! Not sure if one or more of your senior staff suffers from a bizarre mental affliction? Check out these symptoms and see if you can make a match!

- *Agoraphobia.*   Fear of open public places and crowds. Now, what could be more open, or more crowded than your office on a Monday morning? If you have been an employee of the company for the past 10 years and have yet to actually *see* the person who signs your paycheck, you've got yourself either one shy person or a closet agoraphobic.

- *Obsessive-compulsive.*   And you thought there were no more bargains! Two for one. On the obsessive side, this person is the one who is plagued by recurrent ideas and fantasies (like manufacturing a car that runs on fermented garbage), and if that isn't bad enough, the compulsive side makes him or her form task teams to try and make the idea work! This person feels that this also benefits mankind by disposing of unwanted litter.

- *Narcissistic personality.*   Mirror, mirror on the wall . . .Who is the greatest CEO of all? Me! If you can hear this speech when passing by the head person's door (full-length mirrored door), it's a fair assumption that you are dealing with someone who has no trouble describing his or her better points.

- *Avoidant personality.*   They love me, they love me not. Why don't they love me? Would they love me if I gave them longer lunch hours? This is the person whose puppy bit him or her as a child, whose teacher said would never amount to anything, and who was always picked last in sports. In business the avoidant personality is tough to deal with because the smallest word or gesture may be construed as a personal rejection of your boss and lead to a business life that would make boot camp look like a walk in the park! (My advice is to avoid contact as much as possible and make absolutely sure you attend the company Christmas party.)

- *Masochism.* A desire to suffer, be humiliated, or tortured. Usually done by senior management to those below them.

- *Sadism.* Deriving pleasure from inflicting pain on others. Some sadism practiced by senior managers in this category is overt; some is covert. Examples include having to wear degrading badges with pictures of yourself in which you look like a serial killer; or standing in long lines for the cafeteria gruel of the day, getting to the cashier, paying good money for the stuff, and hearing your name over the PA system calling you to go immediately to the production floor for an emergency. (A mixed blessing.)

- *Manic depression.* This is another two-for-one combination. I think I have had one or two of these over the years as clients. They are the type who are completely in sync with the concepts and plans for the quality improvement process and are your biggest supporters. They are enthusiastic, committed and happy with you, your work, and the results. Then you show up one day, smiling and ready to proceed and BANG! Mr. Congeniality becomes the monster from the black lagoon. Like something out of "Invasion of the Body Snatchers," you would swear that some alien life force took that sweet, happy person and made a miserable, negative duplicate.

Any corporation can find a number of reasons why it is too unique to undergo an improvement process. As long as it accepts these excuses for doing business as usual, it will continue to function as an organization of the competitive world market of 1950 and 1960. The time has come when customers are no longer willing to compromise products and services, and when quality and reliability are more important than cost.

The value of a product or service goes beyond its initial delivery and acceptance by the customer. The hard lesson has been, that in many products, the quality wears off before the label, and the customer is left with a less expensive, but unusable product. More and more, intelligent consumers have begun to realize that the cost of the product itself needs to be weighed against quality, reliability, and performance criteria.

For a long time, companies believed that what customers really wanted was cheap products and that is what they sold. Where companies felt the error of their ways was in customer returns, product recalls, and warranty repairs. The bottom line is that there are no valid reasons why quality improvement cannot be implemented in every corporation and why every customer should not expect, and receive, the best.

CHAPTER 3

Quality Improvement—
The Myth

There arc many myths surrounding the issue of quality improvement. Before senior management embarks on the improvement process, let's examine some of the reasons why many quality improvement programs fail.

● Myth Number 1—The House on Shifting Sand Theory

For the improvement process to take hold and sustain itself over time, there must be a support structure that will monitor, augment, and align the improvement within the organization. For many senior managers, productivity measurement programs are used as the basis of a total quality improvement strategy.

Productivity measurement is a quality tool that has limited value when used as a stand-alone program. The value-added comes when the information is coupled with vendor quality, product/service quality, process quality, and customer satisfaction data. In this way, management can make full meaning of the measurement information in a way that benefits the entire organization. Caution should be given against trying to achieve long lasting improvement by instituting a fad program in place of a strategic plan of quality improvement, which brings us to the next myth.

● Myth Number 2–The Panacea of the Month Club

Another way in which quality improvement programs fail is when companies encounter the "Panacea of the month" panic. This occurs when the latest buzz word in quality is implemented to correct all of the corporate quality problems. A good example of this is just-in-time (JIT) as a quality panacea. When companies try to implement JIT without first addressing the quality issues, they frequently encounter the "just-in-time terrors." This is a terminal disease that corporations get when management chooses the fast, exotic route versus the slow, methodical one. The myth here is that if you put *any* potential improvement program in place within the organization total quality improvement will result. Not only is this a myth, it is the antithesis of the meaning behind total quality and sustained improvement. What the corporations will see as a result of implementing JIT as a stand-alone improvement program is something like this:

- Difficulty meeting production schedules due to poor quality raw material.
- Rise in inventory due to work-in-process scrap.
- Lack of process predictability.
- Vendor delivery problems that are ultimately passed on to the customer.
- Line shutdowns due to process, operator, scheduling, and design problems.

Only when the quality and customer satisfaction issues have been addressed and resolved in every facet of the organization can JIT be optimized as an improvement program. Only when it is linked with a solid vendor certification program, with process controls in place, and management and workers committed to the overall improvement vision, can it succeed.

● Myth Number 3—Beheading for Dollars

The myth that the fastest road to quality improvement and corporate survival lies in the paring down of the organization has its basis in the idea that improvement equals cost reduction and that "chopping heads" is the way to increase the bottom line. This strategy amounts to the same logic as treating the symptom while the patient dies.

Typically, the problem underlying customer dissatisfaction and product/service quality has little or nothing to do with the sheer number of individuals in the organization. Most often, the reasons for lost sales and customer complaints are due to the issues surrounding fitness-for-use, reliability, customer service, and delivery.

Cost reduction and quality impovement can be accomplished simultaneously in a well-defined, well-executed plan that will service the customer at low cost without significantly reducing the work force. Reducing the work force to realize a bottom line savings will not cure the problems of scrap, rework, out-of-control processes, or inferior products and services. Learning to use the work force in a way that capitalizes on its strengths and maximizes its productive participation in the organization is the key to accomplishing a positive corporate bottom line month after month and year after year.

● Myth Number 4—The Making of a Quality Professional: Just Add Water and Stir

Some companies embark on a quality improvement process and make all of the necessary moves for a successful outcome, taking care to educate, train, and plan for quality improvement only to commit "implementation suicide."

Somehow, as senior managers in responsible positions, it is easy and logical to see that key management positions must be staffed with highly trained professionals, skilled in their disciplines, who have exhibited a proven track record of successful performance in their field. Why then, do we develop brain dysfunction when we select the key individuals who will lead the quality improvement/customer satisfaction process?

When we examine the employment criteria for a vice president of any of the other disciplines within the organization, a degree in the discipline and substantial experience in implementing the skills of the job with success as well as management experience are required. Often this practice is not used in choosing the quality leadership of the organization and this is where the problem of successful implementation begins.

When management have made the commitment to focus on quality and continuous improvement through superior customer satisfaction and have put the resources of time, money, and manpower in place to secure the success of the process, this is the critical time for follow through. Unfortunately, this is also the most common place for implementation suicide to occur, and the logic of staffing key quality positions with trained quality professionals is not practiced. The idea that we can make quality professionals like we make instant breakfast drink is never more real than when we choose members of the organization from marketing, manufacturing, human resources, or the financial disciplines, wave the corporate wand over them, and set them in motion to lead what has been designated the most important strategic process.

When organizations commit this type of error, they have not only committed a corporate faux pas, they have betrayed themselves and their customers. By not using the best resources to ensure that the customer receives the very best products and services the organization can provide, we have compromised ourselves by not putting the customer first. We have violated good business logic by having ill-equipped people leading a critical improvement process. We have violated our professional standards for the sake of money, convenience, time, etc.

We are a nation of specialists and experts. As consumers we use experts daily, from medicine to mechanics, and yet the same people who wouldn't call on their stockbroker to perform open heart surgery will play Russian Roulette with their organizations from a quality improvement standpoint. The answer to optimizing the success of company-wide quality improvement does not lie in ordaining some group as quality professionals, but rather in actively pursuing and hiring qualified, experienced quality leaders.

Some would argue that quality engineering professionals can be cultivated from within the organization. Tomatoes are cultivated, quality engineering professionals are not. They come to the work force the same way professionals come to be in positions of authority and responsibility; they earn the right through formal education, demonstrated ability, and proven track records of success in the quality field. As with all professional disciplines, the process of attaining superior skills is accomplished over time and cannot be recreated in a few weeks or months.

If we fail to recognize the role of quality professionals in the organization, we have breached the first criterion of success in achieving world class quality; we have not built an organization of superior people in all disciplines.

CHAPTER 4

Quality Improvement—
The Magic

● Divesting of the Old Ways

If the goal of world class quality is to be achieved in a systematic and committed way, divesting of the old way of doing business and a change in the current culture need to take place. Once the intellectual and emotional commitment is made to produce superior products and deliver outstanding customer service, the process of preparing the organization from a sociotechnical standpoint begins.

The first step of the preparation process begins with an examination of the present culture to determine if the management style is static or dynamic, and whether it promotes change or encourages complacency. The challenge then becomes moving the organization from a static to a dynamic state.

In static, or status quo management, management *inform* rather than challenge, *authorize* rather than empower, and *lead* rather than inspire.

The dynamic or proactive management style results in a work force that *creates* rather than corrects, *innovates* rather than maintains, and *anticipates* rather than reacts.

To create and empower a dynamic work force through dynamic management is only half of the solution. Focusing and directing the strength of the organization in achieving world class quality status is the second half.

As an aid to posturing the organization for optimization of the quality improvement process, the use of improvement dynamics management (IDM) techniques must be understood and practiced.

● Improvement Dynamics Management

IDM is a tool used in creating the organizational climate necessary for success at all levels of the organization, from senior management to the work force. It involves the systematic implementation of a methodology that promotes and rewards internal and external customer satisfaction and discourages the "numbers" mentality. It is based on quality, reliability, and personal pride.

In implementing IDM, there are five basic elements which provide the infrastructure necessary to optimize the improvement process in every level of the organization. These five key elements are:

1. *Authority.* Most often, executives confuse the notion of responsibility with authority. Usually, it ends up that managers have one or the other but not both. For IDM to work, each manager must have both the authority and the responsibility to produce superior goods and services on time and at low cost.

2. *Accountability.* Along with authority and responsibility comes accountability. Managers must be held fully accountable for their decisions and the performance of their departments. To ensure success, the senior staff must provide all of the necessary tools, including financial information to the manager. Full latitude must be given to allow managers to have control of and be a positive influence in their departments.

3. *Rewards system.* To move from a "make the numbers" system to a true world class quality posture, the internal rewards system must be revamped. It is clear that in most organizations it is the number of goods and services delivered versus the

quality of the goods and services delivered that forms the basis for the corporate rewards system. It is also clear that the rewards system influences the behavior of the employees and is key to achieving the desired quality outcome. Knowing this, the following steps should be taken for success:

a. The rewards system must include quality assurance measurement criteria.

b. Quality measurement criteria must be tied directly to the overall business plan.

c. Performance quality must include measurements for both the internal as well as the external customer.

d. The quality performance measurement system must be quantitative and tied to profit, market share, sales, customer satisfaction criteria, and operating expenses.

4. *Profitability.* To maximize total corporate profitability the idea of "divide and conquer" must be practiced. In dividing and conquering for profit, each department is set up as a separate profit center for daily operations and performance measurement purposes. In this manner, each department will be both an internal and external customer of the corporation. A word of caution about the divide and conquer approach: While this method is useful for attaining a dynamic organization indicative of a superior world class producer, the communication lines between departments must be strengthened and full disclosure encouraged and practiced. If we are truly to look at each department as an internal customer of the other department, useful, accurate information must pass freely from one department to another. By keeping each part within the whole at optimum level, we ensure total corporate wellness. With this system, each department builds strength, maintains control, and can measure its own performance at any point in time.

5. *Feedback.* How to give and receive feedback is an important element of IDM. It is definitely a case of quantity and quality. Feedback should be ongoing, complete, and nonthreatening. With adequate feedback, there is no room for rumor, speculation, and anxiety over the unknown. The internal and external department feedback should focus on issues, not people, and should not be used as a forum for witch hunts, public floggings, or "buck passing." It should be used to measure departmental performance and to raise the problems of the corporation to the level at which they can be resolved. One more thing about feedback: Much of the feedback given to managers and workers is negative. This type of feedback is usually used as a weapon rather than as a leverage for improvement, and it generally leaves the receiver feeling defensive, betrayed, and de-energized. "Packaging" the delivery of bad news in such a way that is direct and speaks to the issues while depersonalizing them is more useful than the straight "Rambo" approach. One form of feedback that is underutilized by the static management of average companies is positive feedback. As a group we use positive feedback or positive reinforcement more often with our pets than with our colleagues. This is a powerful tool in feeding the personal needs of the superior work force and dispels the myth that the consistently superior performer does not need or want praise. Positive feedback also sets a balanced environment in which people can get a "real time" assessment of a good idea or solution to a problem. It encourages and verbally rewards excellence and supports the more structured yearly performance appraisal system.

The results of implementing IDM in the organization are as follows:

- Corporate vision *not* tunnel vision.
- Planned management *not* crisis management.
- Communication *not* isolation.

In this type of organization, senior staff, by letting go of some of their day-to-day control, can focus on the critical business issues and plan for the future. Additionally, the system allows managers to truly get back to managing programs and developing their staff. The role of manager is changed from that of expediter/doer to planner, and enhances the value-added contribution of managers as creators.

Direction of the Strength of the Organization

The second half of IDM is the actual implementation. With strengthened communications, the right people in the right jobs, and the necessary quality rewards system, we can begin to look at the elements of IDM as they fit together to form the superior organization.

In a world class quality environment, perfection and total customer satisfaction are the ultimate goals. Knowing full well that people are fallible, the idea is to recognize and systematically remove all of the obstacles that inhibit or prohibit achieving the optimum result. Doing this well requires a delicate balance so that creativity and individuality, ego and innovation are not only preserved but encouraged.

When the "divide and conquer" approach is taken and the remaining four components have been put into place, an internal customer measurement system must be established. This means that if we consider ourselves customers of each other in order to measure our performance, we need to have an internal customer measurement system in place.

IDM uses both work flow analysis and value analysis techniques. Beyond the standard value analysis (where each task has a numerical "value" based on its importance to the end product or service), a numerical quality rating system is used to score the numerical quality performance of each individual performing a task. The quality rating system identifies the level of quality excellence achieved in doing each task right the first time.

In addition, the system involves a method of quantifying performance appraisal documentation in terms of quality, cost effectiveness, delivery, and customer satisfaction to name a few.

These three techniques are linked together to provide a total score indicating performance and detailing the rate of improvement by individual and task. Typically, the rewards system is linked to a *numbers mentality* of how many products/dollars of service delivered and the quality of the delivery is subjective or intuitive. In the IDM system, quality and service are fact- and data based and serve as a truer measure of performance and become the method by which the Corporate Rewards System functions.

Work flow is evaluated to optimize cycle time, handling, cost, and human factors engineering considerations. In the human factors evaluation, criteria such as ease of equipment use, lighting, noise levels, work-station layout, etc., are considered.

Next, value analysis of both primary and secondary functions in each department is conducted. Each function is rated based on importance and reliability criteria. Critical measurement areas are identified and a matrix system is developed to collect data.

In IDM, corresponding quality criteria are created and a numerical quality value is assigned for each primary function identified in the value analysis. Quality data on critical functions are collected to determine specific quality performance against a predefined plan. After quality data are collected, they are evaluated to target areas for corrective action. A corrective action plan is developed for both short- and long-range problem resolution. Corrective action is conducted and periodically monitored to verify its effectiveness.

To stay on target with the vision of the corporation, IDM is directly connected to the corporate strategic plan. IDM uses a data-linking application which allows all of the department managers and senior staff members access to data being collected. This provides a closed-loop system. It also allows workers to check their levels of performance and institute improvement at frequent intervals before major problems occur. In short, it is a system that allows people to identify potential areas of concern before they become areas of major crisis. The system provides feedback for managers and workers to assess individual and departmental performance. Finally, it ties directly into the corporate vision through the strategic plan.

This system of internal customer satisfaction measurement begins with a review of the departmental organization charts and the identification of groups in the following manner:

- Identify all groups to which you are a supplier (of goods or services).
- Identify the specific product or services you supply to each department.

When this has been completed, repeat the above steps substituting the word "customer" for supplier. From this information, you can rate *your* internal customer as well as your internal supplier.

Now, I am about to suggest a radical approach to supplying your internal customers with what they want, when they want it: *Ask.* No, I am not referring to a particular software by the same name. I am referring to doing it the simple, old fashioned way— the way they did it before computers, videos, and answering machines. Simply ask them some of the following basic questions:

1. What information do you require on an ongoing basis from me (my group) in order to do your job (i.e., data, reports, etc.)?

2. What format is best for you to use this information simply and efficiently?

3. How often do you require the information/report and how do you intend to use the information supplied?

4. What level of information is required to meet your needs?

5. Will you require some analysis of the information or will the information itself be enough?

6. Give examples of the type of graphics you prefer to augment the information supplied.

7. Give the group a list of who within the organization and who outside the organization will be receiving this information?

8. Will cumulative data/information be required, and if so, how should the data be cumulated (i.e., weekly, monthly, yearly)?

9. Will an information summary sheet highlighting the major findings/solutions be required?

This list of questions is not meant to be all inclusive, but rather to serve as a suggestion of the type of basic information needed from internal customers so that the probability of supplying exactly what they want, exactly when they want it, will be extremely high. Taking the guesswork out of supplying the right product or service at the right time should be done for the internal customer in exactly the same way it is done for the external customer. *Ask* what customers want, how they want it, what their intended use of the product or service is, and finally, when they expect delivery.

Rate your internal supplier on the following criteria. Use a scale from one to five to signify worst to best, respectively.

1. Response time to customer needs.	1	2	3	4	5
2. Quality of supplied product/service.	1	2	3	4	5
3. First-time-error-free product/service.	1	2	3	4	5

4. Reliability of product/service.	1	2	3	4	5
5. Usability of product/service.	1	2	3	4	5
6. Availability of product/service on demand.	1	2	3	4	5
7. Consistency of quality of product/service.	1	2	3	4	5
8. Level of detail (service).	1	2	3	4	5
9. Availability of supplier to provide/ clarify problem solving solutions.	1	2	3	4	5
10. Competence level of supplier.	1	2	3	4	5
11. Clarity of communications between customer and supplier.	1	2	3	4	5
12. How would you rate your internal supplier's attitude when dealing with you or your group?	1	2	3	4	5
13. Confidence level in the data supplied to the customer.	1	2	3	4	5
14. Is the customer familiar with the origin of the data supplied by the supplier?	1	2	3	4	5
15. Is analysis of data given to the customer?	1	2	3	4	5

Based on your answers to this questionnaire, what suggestions would you have, as an internal customer to help your internal supplier provide a more useful, usable quality product or service? Be specific.

_____

_____

_____

_____

Rate your internal customer on the following criteria. Use a scale from one to five to signify worst to best, respectively.

1. Customer ability to identify needs.   1   2   3   4   5

2. Customer's understanding of supplier's job.   1   2   3   4   5

3. Does the customer have realistic expectations?   1   2   3   4   5

4. Does the customer provide feedback to the supplier?   1   2   3   4   5

5. Is the customer consistent with requests?   1   2   3   4   5

6. Is the customer willing to compromise/meet the supplier half way?   1   2   3   4   5

7. Are customer deadlines easy to meet?   1   2   3   4   5

8. Is the customer involved in your process?   1   2   3   4   5

9. Are customer problems voiced directly to the person supplying products/services?   1   2   3   4   5

10. Does the customer provide enough specific information to get the job done quickly?   1   2   3   4   5

11. Are there open lines of communication between the customer and the supplier?   1   2   3   4   5

12. Does the customer have a
standard format for reports which
he or she has provided to the
supplier?   1   2   3   4   5

13. Does the customer notify the
supplier in ample time regarding
changes to deliverables?   1   2   3   4   5

14. Overall, how would you rate the
quality of the relationship you
now have with your customer?   1   2   3   4   5

Based on your answers to this questionnaire, what suggestions would you have, as an internal supplier, to help your internal customer provide better input to your process and improve the overall quality of the output? Be specific.

_____

_____

_____

_____

_____

_____

_____

There are two bonuses to be realized from using this method with your internal customer. The first one is that you will have a clear understanding of the wants and needs of the customer, as well as a documented "specification" of content, format, and delivery. The second is really a by-product of the first. The up-front time invested in creating this "internal customer specification" can be looked at as a prevention cost to save rework, scrap, and poor customer service non-value-added costs down the road. Often, managers will use temporary help, unscheduled overtime, or outside resources to meet important deadlines and quick turnaround times. Most of the time, this avenue of getting the job done must be looked upon with suspicion, because it represents a warning signal that all is not well in the heart of the organization.

Once armed with the wants and needs of the internal customer and with all of the right people mobilized to make it right the first time, the work is executed. Now comes the moment of truth. Did we in fact meet the internal customers' needs in a quality way? This is where the internal customer performance measurement system comes in. Again, I will remind you of the basic rule of thumb: When you really want to know, *ask*! Of course if you invoke rule number one you must brace yourself for rule number two which says that if you ask, be prepared to deal with the answer. No one likes to hear bad news, and no one likes to be the bearer of bad news, but that is in the past. In a world class organization, any news, bad or good, has its purpose: to make existing products, practices, and services better. Instead of a "shoot the messenger" attitude, we must embrace the messenger, take careful note of what he or she is telling us, and act accordingly.

● Quality as a Strategic Business Plan

Corporations that approach the customer satisfaction philosophy through quality enhancement and superior service must address the quality issues as part of their strategic business plan. Quality goals, linked to the overall vision of the company, should be detailed in the strategic plan, complete with measurable objectives. Positioning oneself from a quality improvement standpoint in the strategic business plan will define the quality and customer satisfaction pieces of the business over a three- to five-year period and will form the basis of the construction of individual departmental quality improvement and customer satisfaction measurement programs. Including quality in the strategic business plan links it directly to the corporate business vision and solidifies the corporation's commitment to promote and deliver quality goods and services.

The act of specifying quality requirements within the strategic business plan gives credibility to the verbal and written slogans espoused by the corporation and places them concretely in the forefront of management as a responsibility to be acted upon, rather than talked about.

Giving quality its rightful place at the highest level of the organization through strategic business planning serves to keep quality goals of the corporation in full view of those in power. It can serve as a method of tracking the progress of quality business implementation over the short- and long-term.

The business of quality requires defining the elements that will govern the manufacture of goods and services to create a superior position in the marketplace. Establishing these elements and measurements for improvement quantifies the goals by which products and services will be created and customer satisfaction measured. It outlines a plan of attack for capturing market share through advanced technical and managerial techniques, structured within a financial and metrics base.

In quality through strategic business planning, the result is quality by design not quality by default. It is customer satisfaction through precisely defined product and service excellence based on customer input. In strategic planning, the quality and customer satisfaction plans become core pieces of the overall business vision, linked to the marketing, sales, human resources, finance, purchasing, engineering, and customer service departments. As the heart of the strategic plan, quality feeds each of the interrelated departments of the corporation. Together, quality and the strategic plan combine to form the high-tech machine called successful business enterprise.

In the past, quality was good press. Today, it is good business. It is the most powerful tool available to corporations looking for a way to rise above the mediocre expectations of the sixties and seventies, and to meet the challenge of the nineties.

● Quality as a Marketing Strategy

Making quality products and delivering quality services is only one part of the battle for customer satisfaction. Bringing the best goods and services to the public in a way that makes them eager to buy is a mixture of art and science. The balance between Hollywood glitz and hard facts is a difficult one to attain when trying to find the best packaging to sell a product or promote a service.

Much of today's advertising is filled with promises of happiness, success, wealth, and romance. It is long on fantasy and short on fact. Marketing in the eighties has packaged our dreams in celluloid and brought them from the boardroom directly to our living rooms, complete with technicolor and Dolby® sound. We are besieged by advertising on television and radio, in magazines, and on billboards with marketing techniques geared to appeal to our senses of sight and sound, and to challenge our most stubborn reserves of consumer willpower.

We, as consumers, have been inundated with the slick presentation of images, real and surreal, produced and directed by Fifth Avenue dreamweavers and have experienced the disappointment that comes from buying the package, opening it up, and finding nothing of substance inside.

The 1990s are about substance versus rhetoric and fact versus fiction. We, as producers of goods and services, will be facing the most sophisticated, informed public of our time and we must be equipped as marketers to appeal to this new audience. Where promises were sufficient to close a deal in the eighties, facts and performance will sell products and services in the nineties.

One of the most powerful tools available to corporations has also been one of the most underutilized in the last decade. Positive data on quality, performance, and service, generated by corporations has, for the most part, remained a deeper, more closely guarded secret than their newest technological breakthrough. In the past, quality excellence and customer service, though cause for much internal hype and celebration have seen little or no exposure to the public by marketing management as a means to broaden the customer base. We are quick to share financial data in our quarterly report with stockholders, to share new product introduction information and new service descriptions with customers and potential customers, but few companies publicize their quality, performance, or service data for public consumption.

Dorothy in the *Wizard of Oz* had the power to make her desires a reality with her ruby red slippers. She was, in fact, always in control of her own destiny and never needed the intervention of wizards and witches to get back home to Kansas. So it is with U.S. corporations.

The marketing managers of American corporations possess a weapon more powerful than the wonder of giveaways, promotions, and discounts. It is quality, pure and simple, straightforward and real. It is the power that comes from making the best, selling it at a profitable, competitive price, and being confident about its reliability in use. Superior companies will seize the opportunity to market quality for profit and get all of the mileage possible out of capitalizing on corporate awards in recognition of quality and superior service. Press releases regarding quality excellence and innovative customer service techniques will replace the fantasy "come-on" approach with tangible value-added for dollars spent. Fact will replace fiction and substance will replace fluff. In quality for profit, the marketing strategy is to "let the performance of the product or service sell the customer."

CHAPTER 5

The Customer Is You

● Customer Satisfaction—The Litmus Test of Performance

Each of us has an internal grading system which we use to determine how well or poorly we perform. For some of us, it is the *praise gauge*, that is, how many "atta boys" or "atta girls" you collect, what monetary rewards you reap, and what corporate perks you enjoy. For the praise gaugers, a happy customer is measured in stock options and leather interiors. Like the market, those customer satisfiers can disappear overnight if not closely monitored and your leather coach can turn into a pumpkin at midnight.

For others, performance and customer satisfaction is measured by the *silence slide rule*. No news is good news and no angry customer phone calls equals contented, satisfied customers and good performance. The name of this game is keep a low profile and do a good job, and the system that produces good products and services is its own reward. Anyone who believes that silence is golden has never heard of the calm before the storm. Silence should never be construed as contentment. On the contrary, in many cases it is the final statement from the terminally discontented. It means that all the avenues of discussion, interaction, and corrective action have netted zero and the customer has countered with a final act of defiance and taken his or her business elsewhere. It is imperative that time is taken to separate the happy wheat from the disenchanted chaff.

The silence quotient is really about the absence of data because it is based on intuitively knowing what the internal and external customer desires and by virtue of the lack of negative information, we assume that all is well. Much of this book pertains to the collection and analysis of data. The importance of hard data in the determination of customer satisfaction levels cannot be stressed enough.

Some companies create a built-in silence quotient in their customer service departments by creating and fostering processes and data systems that react to customer complaints/inquiries in a time span somewhere between next year and never. Have you ever experienced a problem trying to straighten out a billing error? Have you ever been told that "the updated information on billing is being entered on the computer as we speak," and (here's the catch) "the correction will not be realized by our system for approximately 45 days so if you should receive another notice in the mail, please disregard it, thank you." I recently experienced the following problem with a major long distance telephone carrier. See if this doesn't (forgive me) ring a bell with you.

A billing error occurred after an initial billing error that resulted in my being billed for someone else's calls on a phone that I had disconnected the year before. Are you still with me? Now comes error number two. My payment was applied to an account I no longer have, but which belongs to some college students from various parts of the country who were all suffering from homesickness. The students who weren't homesick were calling their boyfriends (or girlfriends) on the West Coast. So there you have it, a telephone bill bigger than the national debt! Which brings me back to the customer service person's advice to disregard the second notice. Surprise! Your account is now sent to a collection agency and you become embroiled in the Customer Service Triangle of Terror. The Customer Service Triangle of Terror is much worse than the Bermuda Triangle. In the latter, you are a blip on the radar screen followed by empty space and death is quick and merciful. In the former, you take all of the time, energy, aggravation, and confusion you experienced with the original company and multiply it by three. Death is slow and painful, and sometimes murder is the only way to speed up the proceedings.

One way to turn the Triangle of Terror into the Square of Suicide is to engage an attorney on your behalf. Now customer service takes on a whole new meaning. The gloves come off and we start learning new customer dissatisfaction language like civil suit and counter suit, punitive damages, defamation of character, and mental anguish. We also learn about court costs and associated fees. For those of you who have not had the agony, let me explain that "associated fees" usually means that your lawyer had to personally visit the home office of the company and three customer service divisions in Europe for a week to get your case ready and must have stayed at Buckingham Palace by the size of the expenses portion of the bill. Add a first class round-trip ticket on the Concorde and you're looking at $20,000 plus change to solve a $600 error. How do *you* spell ROI?

In the meantime, your credit rating has hit rock bottom and you have now been placed in the computer of some major credit agency for the ultimate customer nightmare. But all is not lost. The good news is that under the Freedom of Information Act you are entitled to view and update your file to make corrections/clarifications to your account. The bad news is that the original negative credit rating stays on your file for seven years. More bad news — these credit agencies *never* lose a file!

The third measure of customer satisfaction is the *customer cacophony* or *big noise sensor system*. In this system, measurement of customer satisfaction is made only during the "customer scream cycle." Length of scream, decibel level, and content are considered when trying to determine severity of injury and appropriate corrective action. Another consideration is customer identity. If the customer is a small user of your product or service he or she may experience the entire gamut of customer bashing indignities, beginning with the "unintentional disconnect" when the customer serviceperson inadvertently slams the telephone down in the customer's already irate ear. Of course, these calls are not counted by customer service personnel as dissatisfied customers because they were unable to get enough information on the triplicate form before the customer was cut off.

If you survive the unintentional disconnect, you are ready for the "bait and switch." In the bait and switch, a new, more rational customer serviceperson speaks with you and apologizes for the previous inconvenience and asks you to please repeat your problem to him or her. Fifteen minutes later, just as you are about to believe your problems will be solved, you are told that you will have to speak to someone in authority to get the disposition that you seek.

If you have nerves of steel, the patience of a saint, and a strong constitution, you are ready to enter the customer service home stretch. So mount your steed and get ready for the fiber optic race of your life . . .yes, it's telephone tag! Complete with bad connections, cross talk, and infinite hold buttons. The good news is that if you have come this far, you have proved yourself to be worthy of the stuff that America was made of—perseverance, tenacity, strong will, and a little stardust!

The feelings of the customer regarding customer service, or perhaps the lack of customer service, could best be summed up in a quote from the movie *Network*. In the movie, being plagued by a system that could no longer support nor encourage performance excellence, compelled the main character to invite all those unhappy recipients of the media to go to their windows, open them up, and yell at the tops of their lungs, "I'm mad as hell, and I'm not going to take it any more!"

For those of you who have been in your ivory towers for the last 10 years, let me point out that the consensus of opinion about the quality of goods and services in America has been a firm thumbs down. The difference now is that customers are no longer willing to accept poor products and substandard services or to keep quiet about the hazards they have experienced due to negligence, poor design, and poor safety. When will America learn that cutting corners to save money by compromising quality, reliability, and safety is the quickest way to go out of business? It takes only one critical infraction of the health or safety of the public to initiate a media blitz that will make your business as popular as the plague!

I suggest, that on the next still night, you open your corporate window and listen carefully. That sound that you thought was just the din of spring crickets might well be the sound of some people who are mad as hell.

The exercise of writing down in a journal how managers spend their time is always an interesting discovery of how little time these "key people" actually devote to the job for which they were hired, namely managing a business and the people in it. Another surprise for managers is to discover how little they know about their own people, the vision of the company, and the needs of their customers. Most managers engage in little or no direct customer contact. Some of this thinking can be attributed to the old theory "if it ain't broken, don't fix it." This is sound advice if you are talking about your toaster, but when we discuss the people we lightly refer to as our "greatest assets" (internal customers) or, God forbid, as our "bread and butter" (external customers), this thinking is about as modern as hoop skirts.

Then there is the other side of the coin. Those managers who engage in customer contact based on the "squeaky wheel theory." If the problem is really that big, someone will complain at such a high level of the organization that the manager will be brought in to calm the storm. Wrong again, pinhead! Think about the last time you were so angry with a product or service that you demanded to talk to a manager. I would guess that you were not looking for hand-holding and a good ear, but to GET RESULTS OR RIP LIPS! I strongly advise managers who find themselves in the position of having to deal with irate customers to approach them as one would a wounded grizzly bear. Approach with caution and be prepared to meet your maker if you should anger the animal further.

The simplest way to avoid getting mauled in the woods is by making friends with the bear. Understand that the bear and the human were intended to coexist in harmony and can, in fact, do just that if the humans just exhibit a little respect for the bear. Cheating the bear out of what rightfully belongs to it will cause the bear to come out swinging. Don't make the mistake of trying to hide while being stalked. This is certain managerial death. Once the bear has the scent, it will hunt until it draws blood! Never live under the delusion that an angry bear will give up without capturing its prey. Hiding will only aggravate things further and give the manager the distinction of being a wimp as well as a coward. When you make a commitment to a customer for delivery of goods or services anything less than delivering on your promise is inviting trouble.

● Would I Buy This Product or Service?

A key factor in customer satisfaction success is attitude. Positive attitudes lead to positive actions that end up as positive results. Sound too simple? It is. That is part of the reason why we haven't quite mastered the art of doing it right from start to finish. Corporate America has been too busy looking for the secret key or the missing puzzle piece and trying to solve the cryptogram to see what has always been right in front of our faces.

The posture for successful business in the marketplace should be predicated on answering the question "Would I buy this product or service?" It is not amazing to discover that people who manufacture products or provide services often buy from or use the competitions' products and services in their personal lives. What they are saying is that this product is good enough for someone else but not good enough for me. How much better would we be at making and delivering quality, if we thought of every end user as ourselves or our families?

Much of the improvement and success stories around quality and customer satisfaction are made possible through people and accomplished through the personal touch. In an age of electronic wizardry, voice mail, and the most vile of written communication, the form letter, we have somehow managed to sanitize, sterilize, and homogenize the way in which we communicate with one another.

One step to getting closer to the issues surrounding customer satisfaction is to get closer to the products and services we provide in the marketplace. This is not accomplished by barricading ourselves in "mahogany row," but by getting out on production floors, behind counters, and most important, in the front-line positions of direct customer contact.

If the question "Would I buy this product or service?" gets a no response, the next question should be "Why not?" When we examine the why, we are, in fact brainstorming to identify possible dissatisfiers which can then be changed through the improvement process to become marketable advantages. Chances are that the reasons you would choose competitors' products and services over your own will not be unique. The probability of many people in the marketplace sharing your opinion is most likely quite high.

One of the ways in which we can use the internal customer voice in the organization is through establishing a customer satisfaction and product/service quality panel inside the organization. The function of this panel would be to benchmark products and services of the company against competitors and provide measurement data and recommendations in support of their findings. Obviously, this is an easier task in some companies than in others where direct competitors' products and services can be easily accessed.

In the case where this is difficult or impossible, panel members would use the benchmarking technique to compare their company's products and services to those of industry leaders to isolate differences and measure their impact on customer satisfaction and market share. Where possible, panel members should use the products and services of their company and analyze the quality of these products and services along with targeted customers to solicit feedback regarding quality, reliability, and service.

● Quality Function Deployment— Up Close and Personal

Another tool which is useful in bringing the voice of the customer into the corporation is quality function deployment (QFD). Information gathered through the customer survey process along with benchmarks defining the likes and dislikes of customers is used by the company to identify customer attributes. These attributes should be addressed by the engineering, marketing, sales, customer service, and quality departments to increase customer satisfaction levels and ultimately market share.

When these types of data are available to the corporation, each department can participate in the improvement process based on customer concerns rather than customer intuition. By including all of the departments in the customer satisfaction process, a full complement of ideas, perspectives, and solutions can be obtained rather than the usual single-slant approach. The result is that many people have direct knowledge of the customers' evaluation of the product and service, as well as input into the resolution of the problem. The sharing of customer information is also an indicator of how well the internal process is working. Because that process of delivering quality products and services involves all groups, the process of customer evaluation and improvement belongs to all of the departments responsible in delivering those products/services to customers.

The strength of full customer satisfaction does not rest with the customer service or quality assurance departments. It is the shared responsibility of all those who create and deliver goods for profit. It begins at the moment of conception of a new idea and continues through the process of design, prototype, manufacture, marketing, sales, and final delivery. Just as each of the disciplines plays its part in bringing the idea from conception to inception, its role continues in the evaluation, enhancement, and change directed by customers in the marketplace.

● Customer Satisfaction Is a Contact Sport

Customer satisfaction is about knowing the customer's needs, wants, and desires. It's about anticipating what the market will want tomorrow, next month, and next year, and being in a position to provide it. It is achieved through exploration, not confrontation, facts and data, not intuition . . . in short, it is very much a contact sport.

It cannot be stressed strongly enough that there is a need for direct customer contact. It is the only way to truly know how your market thinks. What problems customers have with products and services; what satisfies and dissatisfies them and why. Knowing the *why* can help a company make changes that directly add value to products and services while increasing market share. It is one of the most valuable data gathering processes a company will undertake because it is a measurement of how well or poorly the company has done its job.

Goods and services are valuable as long as there is someone who will buy them and will continue to buy them. Satisfied customers tell others and become extensions of the company's marketing and sales forces. They become free advertisement in the marketplace for increased sales and revenues for good companies supplying superior products and services. On the other hand, dissatisfied customers can damage the reputation of a company and its image in the marketplace, and have a significant negative impact on immediate and future sales. As a supplier of customer goods and services, your job is to keep satisfied customers not only satisfied, but wanting more and to change dissatisfied customers into satisfied ones.

One way not to try to win customer approval is by offering cheap gimmicks in place of quality products and services. Today's consumers are sophisticated enough to know that an offer of a free plastic telephone or a seven carat cubic zirconia cannot take the place of a product that is less than the highest quality at a competitive price. Companies' warehouses are full of "fulfillment" giveaways, gimmicks, and come-ons manufactured to capture the sale, entice the buyer, and appeal to his or her desire to get something for nothing. Everyone knows that there is no such thing as a free lunch, and that you get what you pay for, so invest in your primary product or service, deliver the best for the money, and the customer will come and continue to come for this alone. The rest is window dressing, designed to make up for inadequate goods and services that can't stand on their own merit. The quality companies of the 1990s will be dedicated to enhancing their goods and services, providing the best main course for consumers through genuine improvement, not sidetracking them with subterfuge.

Customer satisfaction is the end result of a great deal of personal commitment, personal pride in products and services, and a personal touch with people.

In an age marked by computers and electronic wizardry, our lives have been condensed from a personal name (identity) to a number (social security) which has come to take the place of face, voice, and limbs. Our voices have been synthesized into customer identification numbers, addresses, and telephone numbers (still more numbers). In short, we have been sanitized, computerized, digitized, folded, mutilated, and spindled, all in the name of progress. Unfortunately, the process has left consumers as nameless, voiceless numbers engulfed in a sea of paperwork, devoid of human contact.

The missing link between American corporations and the customer is the human touch. Twenty-four-hour hot lines, telephone surveys, and personal letters all contribute to the feeling that our customers are someone special, their business is valued, and their repeat business is our reason for existing. To gain a better perspective of our customers, throw away the crystal balls and replace them with first-hand knowledge. This will be the difference between making hit-or-miss products in a vacuum and creating highly desirable products customers want to purchase.

Most companies approach the customer (if they approach the customer at all) as a dreaded obligation. When problems arise, a typical response is to try and satisfy the customer with the minimum amount of effort possible. After all, the complaining customer has already purchased the product or service and is no longer the focus of immediate concern. The shift away from the customer of the past and current customer to the new customer is very real for many companies who only think in terms of the customer of the moment and the new sale.

There are two things wrong with this approach to dissatisfied customers. The first thing is that the company is dealing from a position of weakness, the disadvantage being that it has already failed to provide a quality product or service and all attempts to win the customers' favor are now being made after the fact. The second mistake comes from the shortsightedness of companies that do not concentrate on the customer as a long-term investment for the future. The time in which a company responds to a customer inquiry or complaint, the manner in which it responds, and the degree of personal attention provided may well mean the difference between keeping or losing a customer. Not responding or responding too late will only add fuel to the customer fire. The idea that the manufacturer is there to market and sell but not to advise and service will be all too evident when needs are not met and promises are not kept.

Direct management involvement in customer problems is the best way to show the customer the degree to which customer commitment is practiced by the company. Lack of management involvement in customer service problems is widespread. Companies who take an innovative customer satisfaction approach do not see the customer-company situation as a confrontation worthy of the attention of a heavyweight boxing championship match, but rather as a genuine opportunity to work directly with end users to solve problems, build trust, and improve the overall quality and reliability of goods and services. For true customer satisfaction to take place, there must be an emotional bond between the customer and the company. For bonding to take place, the company must see, feel, and experience the customer up close. The company must begin to think of the customer in a new way—as the driving force behind the company's reason for being. The company must show the customer that attention to detail and a genuine interest in customer satisfaction are more than just words on a company policy statement.

Mobile customer satisfaction units, designed to bring the company to the door of the customer, should replace the form letter of the 1980s. Teams of company support personnel including the engineering, quality, customer service, and marketing areas should be deployed to establish on-site assistance to customers in need of help. By becoming familiar with the customers' physical environment, needs, product application, and degree of satisfaction, companies can use mobile satisfaction units to respond to customer needs and as a fact-finding mission for the company. It is through this type of aggressive customer satisfaction process that the company can learn about the needs of the customer firsthand.

The impact on the customer is tremendous in terms of forming an emotional bond, building trust, and setting the stage for future business. The idea that the company is out there just to provide goods and services without the support structure to go with it if there is a problem down the line is a real fear for consumers, and history shows that the fear is not unfounded.

The more information a company has about its customers, the better able it will be to provide exactly what the customer wants, on time, and at a competitive price with the highest quality and reliability. Customer satisfaction information is valuable only if customers take the time to fill out surveys or respond to telephone inquiries. Mobile customer satisfaction units can provide real-time data-gathering mechanisms for evaluating products in use or services purchased, while providing the personal touch customers desperately desire.

6

Riding the Improvement Wave

● Win-Win Situations—Finding the Perfect Wave

On a sandy beach, on a clear, hot, blue-sky morning, with surf-boards in hand, the corporate line forms to experience the ultimate summer pleasure phenomenon. The corporation is riding the quality improvement wave when all of the components for quality success have been put into place, the problems have been identi-fied and corrected, and the customers are well served. Riding the quality improvement wave requires physical endurance, strict mental concentration, knowledge of the water, and the athletic prowess necessary to stay on top during the entire ride. It is both a skill and a science, wrapped in a little luck influenced by the powerful ebb and flow of nature. Just as the waves can form that perfect curl to bring the ultimate rush to the rider, shifts in the tide and heavy currents can turn the best experience of the day into a life-threatening nightmare.

The caution here is that while caught up in the euphoria of the surfing experience, subtle changes just beneath the surface may go unnoticed. The other problem with riding the wave is that over-confidence often leads to lack of concentration and loss of footing. The bottom line in this situation is that getting to the top of the improvement wave and "hanging ten" is exactly what all of the preparation, hard work, and attention to the customer has been about. The next challenge is staying at the head of the pack and enjoying the ride, but resisting the temptation to relax too much or take reckless chances based on a false sense of security.

● Finding the Comfort Zone— Adjusting the Quality Temperature

Quality improvement is a continuous process. It is not about riding one perfect wave on one perfect summer day. It is about the development and implementation of a set of proven skills that enable one to ride the wave time and time again with the same, predictable, positive outcome. It is the courage to take on something larger than ourselves with the right combination of healthy caution and optimism. It is handling success with enough self-recognition to perpetuate future successes, but with enough modesty to keep our corporate heads from becoming hydrocephalic.

Riding the improvement wave involves attention to the gentle nuances of the sea. Detecting subtle shifts in nature such as a change of wind or a turn of the tide and being able to shift our weight and change position is necessary to steady oneself and stay on course. Observing and listening to customers for changes in attitude and needs, and hints of dissatisfaction can be the early warning signal we must act upon to avoid a wipeout. The ability to shift gears quickly after a customer early warning signal is experienced is essential to the corporation's survival. Quick response time to offset small problems will prevent larger ones from surfacing later as a full blown crisis.

Quality improvement is always a win-win situation because when positive change is implemented, costs are decreased and service improved, benefitting both the customer and the company. From the creation of a positive corporate image to increased market share and an increase in revenues, the corporation will witness the positive effects of delivering superior goods and services throughout the entire business. For the customer, reliability, quality, and superior service will bring the brand name loyalty that some outstanding American corporations have. The winning combination of reliability, quality, and superior service will make believers out of a previously skeptical public. In the 1990s, companies able to produce and deliver excellence in goods and services continually, will be sought after and coveted by the customer, thus creating a win-win situation.

To be in the position of a world class producer and ride the improvement wave, mutual goals must be reached via a two-way dialog between the company and the customer. The dialog must be devoid of the tribal dances, frills, guessing games, and shrouds of mystery that have been the trademark of companies' isolation from customers in the past. The fear of being exposed in front of those whose approval we seek the most must be put into a new perspective based on mutual respect, honesty, and the desire to excel in the marketplace. Improved communications, sensitivity to the needs and desires of the customer, teamwork, and vigilance are key to the great undertaking that lies ahead. The pressures of a strained economy and fierce competition from within and abroad should only serve to deepen our resolve to ride the improvement wave with the best and brightest.

● Resisting Temptation

Once success has been achieved, there are some temptations which may present the opportunity for backsliding and must be avoided if continuous improvement is to take place. Temptation is a powerful emotion that is difficult to ignore as history reminds us. We need only remember the destructive effects of temptation on the inhabitants of Sodom and Gomorrah or the plights of Sampson, Adam, and Pandora to realize how important it is not to fall prey to any of the following:

1. *The Minute Waltz.* Success through the improvement process may lead to the temptation to try and move too quickly, before management and the work force are able to comfortably work with new quality skills. Anticipating the customers' needs comes from practicing the skills of customer data col-

lection, first-hand involvement in customer problem solving, and continuous benchmarking of your company's performance against that of the competition. Simply getting to the marketplace first does not always result in achieving the desired outcome. Getting to the marketplace quickly, with the best information about the customer and the best combination of product and service quality is the winning ticket.

2. *The Tortoise Temptation.*   The tortoise only wins the race in fairy tales. Finding the correct pace in implementing quality in the organization takes time, but not a lifetime. Sometimes the temptation becomes a search for perfection, dotting all of the i's and crossing all of the t's with surgical precision. This technique works well in open-heart surgery, but in real life corporate America it is certain death. Effective management should exercise good business sense in arriving at a cut-off point which is economical and customer value-added.

3. *Looking for Mr. Goodbar.*   The technique of going from one strategy to another doesn't work in singles' bars and it doesn't work in American business. Discovering what works inside your organization is a long, dynamic process and once begun, should continue to evolve to a point of excellence consistent with the corporate business vision. The temptation to lose sight of the corporate vision in favor of shortcuts or fads or to be different simply for the sake of being different will shake the foundation of the corporation. Remember, while you are looking elsewhere, thinking that the grass is greener on the other side, the competition may be mowing your lawn! Using this tactic in business only leads to confusion and loss of focus and could very well move you from the improvement wave to the nearest sand bar.

4. *Biting the Hand That Feeds You.*   Sometimes during the improvement wave experience, we can become so caught up in our own sense of achievement that we forget the people who are responsible for putting us there in the first place. Losing sight of who is essentially paying your salary is losing sight of primary objective number one: "Serve the customer. Don't bite the hand that feeds you!" Most corporations are very short-sighted when it comes to customer recognition. Most workers believe that it is their managers who hold the key to their

success in the business world. For managers, they believe it is the senior staff who will make their destiny. Senior staff believes that the future lies with the CEO. In reality, the customer holds the power to make or break the organization by purchasing or not purchasing, by praising rather than condemning.

5. *The Head in the Sand Approach.*   The search for perfection is not static. It is not something that is attained, then forgotten. It is a lifetime pursuit of action, measurement, evaluation, adjustment, and remeasurement. Our customers are not one-dimensional entities who find that perfect product or service to purchase for all time because it fits their needs (which will never change). The will of the customer is very much influenced by economic, emotional, intellectual, and technological variables. What worked for customers 10 years ago may not suit their needs today. When companies close their eyes to a changing market, a corporate gold mine can quickly become a corporate land mine. Some companies that have experienced the improvement wave may believe they have found all of the answers and no longer need to participate in the company-customer partnership process. Winning one battle is not the same as winning the war. It deserves recognition and should be used to continue the momentum of the improvement process, not as an excuse to stop trying. Putting your head in the sand may be good for the ostrich, but it's hell on the human respiratory system!

● Monday Morning Quarterback— The Value of a Quality Postmortem

The greatest of faults, I should say, is to be conscious of none.
Carlyle, *Heroes and Hero Worship*

To preserve the quality improvement process in the face of adversity is a challenge. To preserve it without destroying everything you have gained in the quality success process is critical to future business. We have all, at one time or another, been in the uncomfortable position of missing an important sign, forgetting a key element, or fumbling the ball on the one yard line of our business careers. The usual reaction to "blowing it" is to expend a lot of time and energy doing one of the following two things:

1. Hiding all the evidence that links you directly or indirectly to the problem, while looking for a scapegoat to take the professional fall.

2. Blaming yourself as being solely responsible and magnifying the problem (and your contribution to it) to the point where it consumes all of your time and energy. This is particularly harmful because it can lead to the destruction of self-confidence and it can paralyze the ability to make future decisions.

Getting past the need for placing blame and beating a dead horse is necessary in order to truly understand and evaluate inadequate performance. By taking the emotion out of the situation and looking at it as an opportunity to examine the facts, it can be more than educational.

Like a pathologist uses information about the life and death of his or her subject to advance medical science, so should we perform a quality postmortem to gain valuable insight into our weaknesses. Our goal is to improve our internal and external operations, as well as to prevent future errors.

If history *does* repeat itself, the problem becomes one of selective repetition, or how to repeat our successes without suffering the embarrassment of repeating our failures. Instead of becoming "once burned, twice shy," it is imperative to become once burned, twice wise!

In the quality postmortem, begin at the beginning with an evaluation of your strategy, market research, quality planning, and execution. Next, evaluate internal product quality and timeliness of delivery. If you score high marks on all of these, chances are that service might be the cause of your problem. Examine the number of service calls, repeat calls, parts availability, and competency of customer service representatives to determine the level of service performance. Response time to the initial complaint, total time to repair/replace the product, and down time experienced by the customer should also be calculated and evaluated.

Data compiled in all of these categories can be used to evaluate customer service representative performance, customer dissatisfiers, and non-value-added costs arising from inadequate and poorly executed procedures. Exposing service weaknesses may also lead to design and manufacturing changes that will result in quality and reliability improvements. For instance, if customer service data uncover a problem related to high infant mortality of a part in the field, a redesign, parts analysis, and reselection or process improvement to weed out weak parts may solve the problem.

In a nonmanufacturing environment, some areas to explore include:

1. Interaction between the customer and the customer service representative.

2. The customer service representative's ability to lower customer anxiety.

3. The time lapse between the customer's inquiry and recognition by a service person.

4. The cycle time to process the customer inquiry.

5. Customer feedback on the status of the inquiry.

6. The cycle time for customer complaint resolution.

7. Followup to ensure that customer satisfaction has been achieved.

In scoring your performance in the area of service, give extra points for innovative customer service and customer service beyond the call of duty. This category includes such items as:

- Taking extraordinary measures involving personal sacrifice to ensure complete customer satisfaction.

- Absorbing a momentary, monetary loss to preserve the long-term company-customer relationship.

When assessing your performance in the area of attitude, give yourself bonus points for all of the following:

1. Knowing and using the customer's name.

2. Superior knowledge of the goods and services provided.

3. Flexibility of customer service people to satisfy the customer in a productive manner by presenting alternative choices/solutions to the problem.

4. Applying superior listening skills when engaged with the customer and using them to initiate problem solving at the customer's initial point of entry.

5. Willingness and enthusiasm to stay with the customer throughout the customer complaint cycle. (This alleviates the need for the customer to explain the problem over and over again to various people within the company before any action can be initiated.)

6. Personal followup on the corrective action taken to continue the customer bonding process.

Deduct points for any of the following customer blunders and make them the target of your internal improvement process:

1. Abruptness with the customer.

2. Putting a customer on hold during a customer complaint call.

3. Insufficient knowledge of the goods or service provided.

You are ready for the Quality Hall of Shame if you are guilty of any of the following:

1. Rudeness to a customer.

2. Placing blame.

3. Making excuses.

Be concise when calculating the final scores for service. Deal with facts not intuition, and approach the exercise as an opportunity to perfect the company-customer connection. List both positive and negative information, balancing what you failed to do, or did poorly with your areas of strength. Concentrate on the areas that need improvement and adjust them with the customer in mind.

CHAPTER 7

The Catalog of Quality Diseases

When we talk about the healthy organization, we mean one which is free of the six deadly quality diseases. No doubt, you are already familiar with the seven deadly sins. The following represents the corporate equivalent — the six ways of quality suicide.

● Anorexia Nervosa—Quality Starvation

In the case of anorexia nervosa, the corporation withers away from quality starvation. In this scenario, the company has speeches, banners, cards, and sometimes even welcome mats espousing a quality first attitude. This overt effort is backed up by a covert implementation of no budget, inadequate staff, and a make-the-numbers mentality. It is a classic case of excellent use of the doublespeak technique.

Unfortunately, the inertia that results from the lack of "feeding the quality machine" is often the result of the CEO's and management's lack of understanding of superior quality and customer service. Conceptually, it is easy to accept and believe in quality first and product and service excellence. Being against quality is like being against motherhood, apple pie, and the American flag, but in practice quality excellence requires more than just the conceptual seed. It requires three well-balanced meals each and every day. Money, qualified manpower, and a clear path to accomplish the tasks at hand are the three basic meals necessary to keep the quality machine humming. Without them, the human body will wither and die of starvation.

● Bulimia–The Quality Binge– Purge Syndrome

Occasionally, you can get too much of a good thing and I have known of organizations with a kamikaze approach to quality that burn themselves out early in the game. This type of behavior is usually followed by a do-nothing attitude that may last longer than the initial quality feeding frenzy—a perfect case of corporate quality bulimia. As is the case with gastronomic delights, there is a big difference between a well-executed gourmet meal and a Roman orgy where quantity, speed, and a no-holds-barred approach is de rigueur. When quality bulimia is used as the method of improvement, one can expect a fabulous feast, followed by a less than spectacular purge, leaving the organization pale, sickly, and less than enthusiastic at the prospect of facing another quality meal.

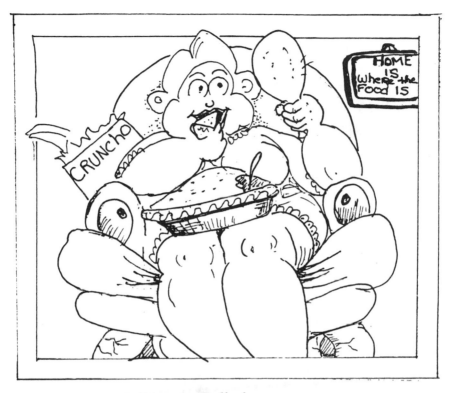

Bulimia

In this kamikaze or "bull in a china shop" approach, quality planning, well-thought-out execution, and implementation successes are put aside in favor of "I want it all now" thinking followed by "I can't believe I ate the whole thing" feeling. Organizations suffering from quality bulimia may end up devoid of strength necessary to turn the corporation around, and like the Roman Empire, disappear from the corporate contenders race into ruin.

One of the most difficult challenges facing the bulimic organization is learning to move forward at a moderate pace and gradually build up speed. The right rhythm and correct level of quality nourishment are reached when the organizational heart gets an aerobic workout, without getting shinsplints. As strength and endurance increase, a new, more aggressive quality workout should be introduced. Steady monitoring of corporate vital signs and more challenging workouts will get better long-term results than weekend warrior athletics.

● Dwarfism—Diminishing the Quality Emphasis

The expression "good things come in small packages" is fitting if you are referring to any of the following:

1. Small, expensive baubles from Tiffany & Company.
2. Bearer bonds.
3. The keys to a new Porsche.

   In most other cases, however, it is an excuse for not providing adequate goods and services. It is the third leading cause of organizational death in the United States. Though many organizations start out with conviction, plans, and goals, they sometimes become sidetracked. Loss of energy (momentum winddown) and dwarfism (diminishing of the quality emphasis) are the end results.

Dwarfism

The cure for dwarfism is not to put Tom Thumb on the rack and pull his little body like a rubber band to make him into Tom Selleck. The goal here is not a revival of the Spanish Inquisition. One of the ways in which we will always know where we are going is to know where we have been. Feedback on progress, setting of new goals, and the constant challenging of ourselves and each other will help sustain the flow of blood through the corporate vascular system. The adrenalin needed to keep the blood pumping is the continued emphasis on quality, with a customer focus.

● Paranoia—Quality-Gate Cover-Ups

Not since the break-in at the Democratic National Convention have I seen such a myriad of "quality-gate" cover-ups resulting from mismanagement, indecision, lack of focus, lack of commitment, and too much customer distance. If organizations spent as much time addressing the ills of the internal system as they do trying to deny them or place blame for them, there would be more superior companies.

Organizations suffering from quality paranoia feel that everything and everybody is keeping them from realizing their dreams. In reality, organizations who suffer from this kind of disease become self-fulfilling prophecies of struggle, failure, and finger-pointing that ultimately lead to witch hunting, conviction, and execution of the "guilty." I should point out that the "guilty" is someone who is below you in the organizational hierarchy, an easy scapegoat, expendible, but *never you!*

Paranoia

Organizations suffering from paranoia and associated "quality-gate" cover-ups have a standard, prepackaged list of reasons why "they" are out to get us, and why goals are never met. It goes something like this:

1. The forecast was wrong.
2. They changed the product mix.
3. The never tell us anything.
4. We didn't have enough:
    a. Time.
    b. Manpower.
    c. Resources.
    d. Materials.
    e. All of the above.
5. Customers don't know what they want.
6. The competition:
    a. Got there first.
    b. Underpriced us.
    c. Both (a) and (b).

When all else fails and accusations, explanations, and whining don't produce the desired results (i.e., getting you/your group off the hook), plan number seven is used as the last resort:

7. Claim you are the victim of a vendetta.

Plan seven is for the manager whose paranoia has gone beyond over-the-shoulder checking for internal spies and has graduated to employing an official "coffee taster" each morning. Rationalizing the vendetta is the second part of plan seven. Remember—when all else fails, claim jealousy. Claim that you/your group are victims of the green-eyed monster. This is particularly effective if you have recently upstaged your boss, are the "fair-haired boy/girl," are a young hotshot, or are married to the daughter/son of the CEO. The result of this type of paranoia and cover-up is a lack of positive energy which should be directed toward the goal of ultimate customer satisfaction and is instead expended in in-fighting.

A footnote to "quality-gate" paranoia and the cover-up disease is that while the staff is busy accusing, responding to accusations, and not taking care of business, they are becoming an excellent target for a hostile takeover. Of course, for the true paranoid, this is the ultimate grist with which to feed an already over-active imagination.

● Euphoria—The "Twinkie Defense" for the Artificial Quality High

This is also known as the devil-made-me-do-it syndrome. When an organization experiences a large quality success, many times the corporate excitement unleashes an army of swelled head quality zealots. Sometimes the resulting mass euphoria creates an artificial quality high.

Like eating too many Twinkies, the quality high is like a sugar rush; it feels great at the beginning, gets better for the short fall, and then crashes. Unlike the bulimic organization, the food (success) is consumed, converted to a heavy dose of glucose, gets expended quickly by the body, and leaves the organization sluggish. The craving for more sugar (quality success) becomes so strong, that quality planning and measurement become secondary or worst case, and are omitted in favor of the quick results path.

Euphoria

When the organization suffers from quality euphoria, the successes begin to turn to failures. Even though the tendency is strong to adopt an "I know it all" attitude and to feel that going through the planning, checking, measuring, and adjusting phases is only for beginners, it is imperative that all of the steps be done all of the time. Shooting from the hip went out with Wyatt Earp. World class quality organizations still load, release the safety, take careful aim, and *then* fire. This way, you will always get your man, or market share as the case may be.

The rule here is the same as in all things: *Artificial anything is never as good as the real thing.*

● Alzheimer's Disease—Amnesia of the Quality Goals

I almost concluded the chapter and forgot to mention the last fatal quality disease: Alzheimer's disease. Organizations suffering from Alzheimer's exhibit a gradual loss of the goal of quality as a competitive edge. I emphasize the word gradual because the goals set

Alzheimer's

through quality planning and strategic market positioning become obscured, rather than deliberately abandoned.

First it's just the small things that are overlooked in the quality process — a forgotten step here, an ignored customer preference there, then gradually the omissions become more frequent until they result in a permanent loss of quality memory. Keeping the mind sharp requires regular challenges of the intellect and the imagination. When intellect and imagination are underutilized, they atrophy and quality dementia slowly takes hold within the organization. Corporate Alzheimer's is particularly insidious because of its gradual nature. Most often, an organization will respond to a radical change of either addition or omission because the change is noticeable enough to evoke a reaction.

In corporate Alzheimer's, the quality goals are eroded away very slowly until their absence results in end product, service, or customer problems of such a magnitude that they can no longer be ignored. The bad news is that by the time the organization becomes reactive, it usually has missed the window of opportunity needed to take new market share or maintain present market share. Some symptoms of corporate Alzheimer's include:

1. A vacant stare when discussing the customer.

2. An overall child-like attitude.

3. A desire to reminisce about everything in the past while remembering nothing about the present.

If you or anyone in your organization is suffering from the above symptoms, emergency medical help is advised.

CHAPTER 8

Managerial Losers—
This Could Be You

We have met the enemy and they are ours.
Oliver Hazard Perry, after the Battle
of Lake Erie, 1813

This chapter is provided for self-evaluation purposes. It will be a painful process that requires total honesty, objectivity, and a strong constitution. If you can identify yourself as one of the following managerial losers, you should do the honorable thing. If you can identify one or more of your coworkers, they should do the right thing. If you can identify your CEO, CFO, or chairman of the board in this chapter, by the time you finish reading it, you will have been the victim of a hostile takeover, gone bankrupt, or (hopefully) moved to another company.

From the beginning, I have emphasized the importance of superior people and superior organizations in becoming world class. By the same token, having low corporate class or no corporate class, thus being out-classed by the competition can be the result of managerial losers. For those of you who are not familiar with the managerial loser, these are the polyester princes, boardroom bores, daytime drones, merger megalomaniacs, and all-around bastard big boys. Let's have a look at the most offensive of the bunch.

● The Recluse— "Not Now, I Have a Headache"

Have you ever worked for or with a manager who was as scarce as a cab in New York City on a rainy day? A manager who could qualify as having a no-show job, or someone whose availability could be compared to getting an appointment to see your doctor on a Wednesday during the height of golf season? If you see "Puksatawnie Phil" more often than this guy, or if you answered yes to any or all of the above, you have had a face-to-face, or shall I more appropriately say a face-to-shadow encounter with the managerial recluse.

Not to be confused with someone who is actually out there in the trenches doing his or her job, and therefore not readily available, the managerial recluse has a disappearing act that would make Houdini envious.

The Recluse

The managerial recluse is a master of the "weave and dodge" technique and possesses the world's longest excuse list for why he or she is unable to:

1. See you.

2. Speak with you.

3. Resolve outstanding issues.

To make getting to the managerial recluse an even more formidable task, he or she often has front line help. Armed with a secretary who is a cross between a pit bull terrier and Brunhilde, he strategically places the "Human wall" between himself and the organization. The pit bull terrier's job is to stall, block, tackle, confuse, and misdirect anyone who might threaten this elusive boss.

A typical conversation with the managerial recluse's secretary might go something like this:

Q. **WHAT YOU SAY:** "Hello. This is John Jones. Is Jack there?"
WHAT YOU THINK: *(Why am I bothering? I can never find him! I wonder where he's hiding this time?)*

A. "Mr. Smith is not available at the moment."
(You haven't got a snowball's chance in hell of getting anything out of me.)

Q. "I'm at the Baker Street plant at the moment and we have a quality problem. Do you know where I can find Jack?"
(I have a better chance of getting Gorbachev to defect than getting any information out of "witch woman.")

A. "I'm sorry, but Mr. Smith is traveling today and is not expected back in the office."
(I love these little power trips, especially when I can play them on the "brass." Jack would get a kick out of the way I'm jerking this person around!)

Q. "Is there any way I can reach him on the road? As I said, we have a pretty serious quality problem and we need to make a final decision right away."
(If I get any more runaround, I'm going to handle this on my own. I know he's out practicing his swing on some golf course!)

A. "I have no way of getting in touch with Mr. Smith now. I believe he is in transit. However, if he calls in I'll give him your message."

(Hmmm, 8:00 AM. He must be "teeing off" at Greendale. I have to cut this call so I can have a coffee break.)

Q. "Would you please make Jack aware of the urgency of the problem and ask him to call me as soon as you hear from him?" *(The odds of him getting any message are slim to none. I'd have better odds at the blackjack tables in Vegas! Maybe Johnson can get in touch with Jack, he goes sailing with him on the weekends. Yeah, I'll call Johnson's office. I hope he doesn't play golf!)*

A. "I will make absolutely sure that Mr. Smith gets your message and returns your call immediately." *(First, I haven't the vaguest idea when he will return. When he returns I'll tell him, but I'm sure he has better things to do than be concerned about what's going on over at Baker Street.)*

A. "Thank you. Goodbye." *(Thanks for nothing.)*

Of course, the recluse will eventually get your message, and (between meetings) will call you back on the "fly" with that same hurried tone that makes you feel as if you had intruded on a private family affair. The recluse will explain that this was the very first opportunity he or she has had to get back to you, and how concerned he or she was to hear of the problem. The recluse is counting on the fact that after this much delay, you no longer need his or her input. He or she is usually right.

Unfortunately, it is difficult to fire the recluse—you can't hit a moving target! The recluse is a liability to the quality improvement process and should be removed from the organization. Maybe a telegram sent to the club?

● The Juggler—He's Got the Whole World in His Hands

When we talk about the "juggler" as a managerial loser, we are really talking about someone who starts out as a hotshot, technical genius, managerial wizard, boy/girl wonder, a master of the art of getting things done.

So, how is the hotshot rewarded for his or her efforts in most organizations? The hotshot is recognized for outstanding ability and performance by becoming the "only one who can take care of":

- Quality issues.
- Customer service issues.
- Operations problems.
- Financial matters.
- Special projects.
- Delicate personnel situations.

People respect the hotshot's leadership abilities, strength under pressure, and logical approach. They want to be associated with the hotshot and the programs he or she works on. They want to be on the winning team. The hotshot develops a corporate cult and delights in challenging both the cult and himself or herself.

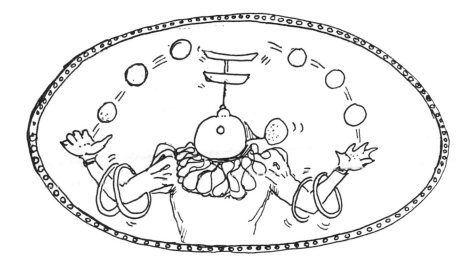

The Juggler

Because of numerous strengths, the hotshot takes on more and more special projects until he or she is no longer the capable, in-control manager. He or she is the "juggler," person of a thousand corporate obligations. A mere mortal, expected to perform super-human feats in record time. A human Gumby, being pulled in all directions by the system until there are too many balls in the air and the juggler starts to lose the rhythm. One by one, the balls tumble down and the juggler is heckled by the crowd. The same people who applauded earlier, now become the angry mob that forces the juggler off the stage.

We all know of managers who are overloaded by the system, spread too thin, and in charge of too much. Ultimately, this corporate machine becomes overtaxed and the quality of goods and services suffers. The words "just say no" also have a place in the business world. Saying yes too many times can end in corporate disaster when the "juggler" experiences frustration and burnout where there used to be accomplishment and the desire to move forward toward the next challenge. When the organization places too much responsibility on the juggler to be planner, implementor, expeditor, hero/heroine, etc., it has made not one, but two mistakes. The first is the abuse of the corporate star, and the second is cheating the remaining resources of the organization out of the ability to meet their professional potential. It invites apathy, complacency, and stifles the involvement and momentum necessary to sustain the improvement process. By developing the technical and managerial skill levels of all of the people in the organization, quality, reliability, and customer satisfaction can be obtained. It is a joint venture, not a solo enterprise.

● Mr. Happy Face—Looking at the World Through Rose-Colored Glasses

The eternal optimist! This is the loser who manages from somewhere other than planet Earth. The yes-man, the good old boy, Mr. Middle of the Road. He lives in the suburbs, has 3.2 children and a dog, drinks milk, and loves everybody and everything just the way it is and wants it to stay that way forever. This person is a happy-face button with feet. No waves, no boat rocking, this person is strictly status-quo. This is someone who would refer to the great flood as a summer shower. This person takes no risks and makes no demands on anyone.

Mr. Happy Face has been with the company since it hung the sign over the front door of the building and he intends to stay right in his little corner office until called out for the gold watch. Mr. Happy Face is a twilight cruiser waiting out the days until retirement and a pension in suspended animation. Occasionally, one is tempted to take his pulse during the mid-afternoon to ensure that he is still, clinically, among the living.

Mr. Happy Face

When considering quality, quality improvement, and world class quality, Mr. Happy Face is bullish on every word, and in meetings on the subject, utilizes the proverbial nod punctuated by the correct number of "sounds great to me's." Perhaps Mr. Happy Face would make a great sidekick for Bozo the clown, but he's like brown Hush Puppies with a tuxedo as far as quality improvement goes. The improvement process requires more time, dedication, and energy than Mr. Happy Face can muster and one of its core elements is change; a word that strikes fear in the hearts of happy-face types all over the world.

The best cure for Mr. Happy Face is to let him realize the dream of retirement earlier than expected. I guarantee that the thought of a canoe, a fishing pole, and some new lures will get his heart pounding faster than the idea of quality function deployment, benchmarking, and life cycle costing. *Bon voyage!*

● Mr. Potato Head—How About a Quality Circle?

What is oval, comes in brown or red and is a good source of potassium? The potato. What is stubborn, traditional, and not open to new ways of doing things? Mr. Potato Head. If Mr. Potato Head is part of your organization, he is easy to pick out of a crowd.

This is a person who still believes that the way to quality improvement is through quality circles and 100 percent inspection. This is the manager who doesn't believe in statistics, automation, computers, or the need to bring the customers' voices into the organization. Mr. Potato Head is certain that this "quality thing" is just a fad that will fade away soon. The idea of expanding quality principles and practices to other departments within the organization is viewed as a grand notion that will never work.

Unlike Mr. Happy Face, who accepts everything without question, Mr. Potato Head questions everything as being *too* something . . . too difficult, too costly, too complicated, too simple, and never doable.

Mr. Potato Head

Mr. Potato Head is fast with the complaints and slow with suggestions on how to make improvements. He always sees the glass as half empty, not unusual for a guy who can best be described as half baked. Mr. Potato Head is an obstacle because he inhibits those who work for him from becoming innovative and from challenging the system. He has little self-confidence and is never a risk taker. If it's not in the book and by the book, there is too much room for potential failure as far as this person is concerned. Thus, staying with the known, even if it is antiquated, it's at least predictable, is the norm for Mr. Potato Head.

When change is proposed, all of a sudden Mr. Potato Head is from Missouri; then it becomes show me beyond any doubt, and the ordeal begins. Remember, there is not enough logic or statistics to change the mind of a stubborn spud.

Unfortunately, the cure for an out-of-control potato is as follows:

1. One jar of industrial-strength mayonnaise.

2. One stalk of celery.

3. One medium onion.

Boil the potato head until tender. Dice into bite-size pieces. Add the remaining ingredients. Toss thoroughly and *voilà* . . . potato salad. Serve with day-old hot dogs and cheap wine. *Bon Appetit!*

● Ivan the Terrible—My Way or the Highway

If you enjoy a good fistfight, brawl, bullfight, or are a diehard fan of the World Wrestling Federation, cockfights, or just plain-old no-holds-barred gang wars, Ivan the Terrible is just your style. If you have daydreams about persecution and keelhauling, you have found your hero in this managerial loser. If raping, pillaging, and/or plundering is your game, and you have been wondering "where all the *real* men are," the answer might be that Ivan the Terrible is alive and well and working in your organization.

Webster might define the word "manage" as "to provide gentle guidance," but Ivan the Terrible doesn't know what the words "gentle" or "guidance" mean. He is Rambo in a suit and tie, a dictator, loner, and iron-fisted tyrant who only knows one way of doing things—his way. Ivan employs the management by intimi-

Ivan the Terrible

dation technique and believes that fear is what motivates people to do the right thing, and, oh by the way, the "right thing" is whatever Ivan decides it is.

For Ivan, a team player is someone on Family Feud. He is less the captain (well, maybe Bligh) and more the imperial ruler. Ivan's office is his castle and in it, Ivan reigns supreme. Ivan's word is law and all decisions are final. There is no such thing as a discussion with Ivan the Terrible because a discussion implies that there is a two-way conversation taking place. With Ivan, it is a monologue in which you are told how it is, what is wanted, and how it is wanted.

Another one of Ivan's characteristics is insecurity. Beneath the macho muscle-flexing lies a mass of vacant brain cells. This is a classic case of too much iron and not enough steam. Because the all-brawn and no-brain leader never is sure of himself or of those who are working for him, Ivan makes the assumption that his own ability is much greater than yours. This way of thinking makes sense to Ivan, because after all, if he weren't smarter and more capable than you, he wouldn't be the boss!

Because Ivan lives in an *us* and *them* world, Ivan also suffers from one of the deadly quality diseases: paranoia. A by-product of this affliction is that in order to make sure that the underlings follow orders to the letter, Ivan wants to be intimately involved in every detail of your work to dot all the i's and cross all the t's. Speaking of crossing things—don't think about doing anything to incite the anger of Ivan the Terrible. This person shows no mercy and takes no prisoners.

To rid oneself of Ivan requires drastic measures and the proven method of choice is as follows: $10,000, a copy of *Soldier of Fortune* magazine, and a touchtone phone. Incidentally, don't worry about the money—you can write it off as a quality improvement expense under "prevention costs."

CHAPTER 9

Managers, Workers, and Customers— The Winning Pyramid

- ## The Vulcan Mind-Meld—Know What Goes On in the Customer's Mind

It takes a great deal of effort to identify customer needs, and to furnish competitive goods and services which fulfill the wishes of the customer, but to accomplish this feat is worth a "corporate place in the sun" in market share and revenues.

In examining ways in which we can get close to our customers, it might be advantageous for us to take a lesson from Mr. Spock. Spock used the "Vulcan Mind-Meld" to probe the deepest recesses of the minds of others in order to become "one" with them. Outside of being a Vulcan Starship officer, or the Amazing Kresgin, there are some signs which can be useful indicators of shifts in the marketplace.

A good example of the recent changes in consumer base and in the demand for and type of products and services purchased is the radical changes in the family unit over the past two decades.

With the dramatic increase of women in the workplace, there has been a shift from a largely male consumer base for items such as housing and automobiles. This has resulted in a change in the way real estate companies and automobile manufacturers market and sell products. The economic influences and social changes that created dual-income families and single-parent households spawned changes in the marketing of leisure goods and services to court the emergence of young, affluent, upwardly mobile "yuppies" with an insatiable appetite for electronic gadgets, gourmet food, and the good life. In single-parent households, day care, fast food, and video games emerged as the most important consumer products and services.

Achieving the Vulcan Mind-Meld does not require having our ears pointed. It does, however, require having them sharpened. As providers of goods and services, we must listen with greater intensity and interest to the voices of our customers through personal contact and ongoing feedback.

Two things were required for Spock to execute a successful Vulcan Mind-Meld: intense concentration and physical touch. Using both of these techniques with your customers will help to achieve the "oneness" necessary for the perfect customer-supplier balance. Intense concentration means the deployment of resources, people, time, and dollars to listen to the voice of the customer and act upon the information received.

For years customers felt abandoned by the companies they trusted the first time they experienced a customer satisfaction problem with goods or services. The consensus was that companies were there to wine and dine, promise and persuade, until the point of cash transaction. Then they folded their tents and stole off into the night — hiding in boardrooms and off-site meetings, courting and wooing the next object of their corporate affection, treating you like yesterday's news.

This type of procedure dealing with customers in need was particularly prevalent with companies who were in the coveted position of virtually being the "only game in town" in a particular product or service. The good news is that this is not as common today because of deregulation of giant conglomerates, increase in technology transfer, and fierce competition in the marketplace. These companies experienced a customer base that was much like a "woman scorned," complete with a long memory and armed with hell's fury. Undoing the wrath of a dissatisfied customer due to price gouging, poor service, or inferior products is a monumental task that even a Vulcan might find too formidable a challenge.

In an era of fast food and fast fixes, companies postured to excel will have to exchange speed for quality, and develop and nurture long-term relationships with their customers. Concentration on customers should not be exercised only in times of trouble. The greatest benefit to be achieved through the Vulcan Mind-Meld is anticipating the customers' needs and genuine interest *before* a crisis occurs. This tactic is a definite change from being brought kicking and screaming in front of the customer to take one's punishment "like a man."

It takes confidence and courage to approach customers in a prevention posture. Facing customers to assess their evaluation of your product *before* they experience a problem can prevent it from happening in the future or lessen its severity should it occur. In either case, you have become greater for the effort in the eyes of the customer and expanded your knowledge of the customer's operation for better service in the future.

In addition to concentrating on the customer by creating a forum in which the customer can be more visible within your organization, there must be physical contact to complete the Vulcan Mind-Meld. The physical touch is a special form of bonding with the customer. It is imperative that customers have contact with the company if the company is to truly serve their present and future needs. This also enables the company to measure its ability to meet those needs on an ongoing basis.

In most companies, the sales force may be the only source of direct contact between the organization and its customers. There are two problems with this: The first is that although salespeople may be excellent sources of information about customers, they are typically not given a formal avenue within the company in which to provide feedback to key individuals within your organization. The second problem is that limiting customer exposure to salespeople alone limits the customer's perspective and may bias data gathering.

Using a customer satisfaction mobile team comprised of several disciplines of the company will be more value-added for both customers and the organization. The balance achieved in using different disciplines in dealing with key customer staff to better understand problems and participate in joint problem solving, provides the emotional bonding and technical credibility necessary to build superior relationships with customers. Mobile customer satisfaction units equipped with diagnostic equipment, computers, and telecommunications tell customers that you are serious about your commitment to them before, during, and after purchasing your product or service. My psychic powers predict that this will be more impressive than a pair of free plastic headphones or a 20-piece kitchen knife set.

Success in the 1990s requires more attention to customer detail than ever before. Corporations must assume a new role in customer relations, based on integrity, mutual benefit and respect. Like good doctors, corporations must monitor the vital signs of the customer, and make sound diagnostic decisions based on test data to provide a lasting cure.

Don't Keep the Customer in the Dark

Another marketing technique which is underutilized by companies is the interest and revenue that can be generated by keeping key customers informed about new products, processes, and innovative customer service approaches. By treating the customer like a best friend instead of an unwelcome relative, sharing new technology process and product development information will encourage the customer to strengthen his or her business association and increase the level of business the customer is doing with the company.

Do more than sympathize! What customers with concerns want to hear is the reason they have experienced a problem and what immediate steps you will take to correct it. Follow-up contact should include the long-term resolution of the problem and an audit of its effectiveness.

I was recently asked to fill out a customer survey at the specialty market where I am a frequent customer. I was told that the survey was being given to assess the quality of goods and services supplied by the company and that they were especially concerned with customer comments on how they might improve the present quality levels and what specific dissatisfiers may have plagued me over the last 12 months. They explained that the survey would take approximately 10 minutes to complete and that I would be compensated in the amount of $5 for my time. Adequate space was provided at a center counter, allowing for ease of performing the task. The questions were specific rather than general and addressed both product and service issues in every department of the store. The person who administered the survey remained present to clarify any questions that may have been unclear and to personally collect the completed surveys and thank each participant on behalf of the company.

Inviting customers into your process will give them an opportunity to contribute and critique your present method of delivering quality in the marketplace. This type of procedure should be implemented at the beginning of a customer-company relationship, once the product is being developed and manufactured and after the product has been delivered. Early entry of the customer in your process can prevent disaster from occurring after delivery and will be a cost savings as well as good public relations.

Arrange a monthly forum in which customers are invited to share specific problems and concerns with key personnel within your organization. This act alone can mean the difference between maintaining the delicate "oneness" with your customer and pushing the customer into the arms of the competition. It is a psychological victory from the customer's perspective to be asked for an opinion and to contribute user input to the company to improve services or products. It sends a message of commitment to excellence and dedication to a continuous improvement policy. It shows that the corporation places the value of the customer above the quick sale.

Sharing information about the internal workings of your company is a bold step. Inviting the customer to participate in the process is a visionary move, only to be undertaken after the corporation has set and practiced standards of excellence in quality, reliability, and service. Current business practice is to deal with the customer at arm's length. Now we must deal with the customer face-to-face. Many will view bringing the customer in to participate in the "process" as too radical. For them, it will be surveys and letters, telephones and customer benchmarking reports (business as usual); limited gains will be made.

How much of what we see at the end of the cycle as customer miscommunication could be relieved by having the customer participate in the company's process? We have already experienced the success that comes from creating such partnerships with key vendors. By getting inside their process, and lending our perspective as customers of their goods and services we have become an extension of their quality and customer service organization and increased our own level of customer satisfaction as an end result.

At the end of the experience, I felt both physically and psychologically boosted. Filling out the customer satisfaction survey reminded me why I chose to shop at the store in the first place and I started to examine the reasons. Let me first explain that there are six markets within three miles of my home, so each is equally convenient.

1. *Convenience*:   All markets equal. Market A, where I shop is the most expensive of the six.

2. *Cost*:   Market A, most expensive; market B, least expensive; market C, moderately expensive; market D, moderately expensive; market E, less expensive than C and D; market F, equal to E.

The quality of products sold at each of the markets varied from fair to excellent. Again, my store (A) had the highest consistent product quality.

3. *Product quality*:   Market A, very high; market B, poor; market C, high; market D, good; market E, fair; market F, fair.

The next issue was service. Up to this point, my choice could have been to shop at establishment C, which has high quality, convenient shopping and is moderately expensive. The shift to selection of market A over market C became a no-contest situation based on the product quality aspect not provided by market C and a definite edge in A over C in customer service. This brings me to the final two categories of consideration: health and safety and customer service.

In the health and safety category, market A began to pull ahead of market C, by providing organic products, unprocessed products, and meat and poultry free of steroids and antibiotics. Vegetables are offered free of pesticides and packaged foods free of salt, sugar, and preservatives. Also excellent was communication to the customer on the purity of foods and their contribution to consumer health and well being. The company that owns market A publishes pamphlets describing the methods of growing fruits and vegetables and the breeding, nurturing, and slaughter of meats and poultry to preserve purity and freshness. In the departments where prepared foods are offered, description of all of the ingredients is posted to aid customers in their selections and to alert them to any possibility of allergy or adverse health reaction for persons sensitive to wheat, lactose, or other food substances.

All of the above most probably would have been enough to increase its customer base, but the company became aggressive and innovative in its customer service approach and I was hooked. In addition to delivering right to your home, carrying bundles to your car, and providing an in-market cash machine, the company provides the following:

- Hours from 10:00 AM to 8:00 PM during the week and on Saturday; noon to 8:00 PM on Sunday.
- One hundred percent refund on any product that does not meet the customer's standards.

The range of hours allows working people like myself to shop in the evening.

Because of the high degree of confidence in the consistent quality of their products, as well as a high priority on the customers' value, the company felt that a refund offer was appropriate.

In the area of employee attitude and competence, market A emerged superior once again. Employees exhibit a pleasant, courteous demeanor and are eager to assist customers in making shopping there pleasant, easy, and painless. In every department, service people are highly knowledgeable of the products they sell. From a discussion of the ingredients, method of preparation, and specialty items, from future offerings to packaging preferences, all of the employees are masters of customer service.

On-site testing of new prepared foods is done with customers as they shop, to get preliminary feedback on quality, pricing, and potential market size. From the on-site information gathered, in addition to the customer survey information compiled during the year, the company implements its internal quality improvement process. All of its efforts have paid off in improved customer satisfaction and repeat business even though its prices are higher than those of other stores. What does this tells us? It tells us that perhaps the need for personal contact, soliciting performance data from customers, and making changes based on customer likes and dislikes is important enough to consumers to keep them coming back.

In consideration of customer concentration and the pesonal touch, there is one more piece of advice: Begin now, before your competition does!

The Vulcan Mind-Meld can be achieved through using the techniques just described and adding some of your own. Be confident that when the customer is cared for, the rewards are great. As Mr. Spock would say, to do less would be completely "illogical." Try the Vulcan Mind-Meld . . . and "live long and prosper!"

● Quality for Profit—Follow the Yellow Brick Road

In their work on quality costs, Philip B. Crosby and H. James Harrington proved that quality and profit do, in fact, mix. The opportunity to become world class in products and services is great and it is real. The yellow brick road does exist and it is paved with the revenue gained from eliminating non-value-added activities, implementing the improvement dynamics management process and measuring performance from a customer satisfaction perspective. Our yellow brick road is paved with gold, not yen, and American corporations will never be successful in America if we simply restructure ourselves and our organizations to mirror Japan.

In our quest for perfect product, the best service and the ultimate satisfaction of our customers, we have neglected to remember who we are. The same traits that made us successful Americans should be used to make American corporations great. Individuality, creativity, innovation, and risk taking have always been the building blocks upon which our greatest successes have been achieved. We are a culture that thrives on healthy competition and individuality. We create, innovate, challenge, and pursue our goals within a unique heritage that should be embraced rather than disregarded.

I am an advocate of both teamwork and individual contribution, of being close to the work and the customer while still maintaining a place of refuge complete with office, door, and window. It is important for managers to have privacy in which to collect their thoughts, destress themselves, and energize their creative processes. Tearing down the walls may work in the Far East, but it can be a nightmare in the West. The most damaging walls are not the ones that surround our office furniture; they are the ones we create between ourselves and our colleagues. They are not made of wood and nails but of our own human frailties.

Each time we approach a problem with a preconceived attitude of failure, we have created a self-fulfilling prophecy of defeat. Each time we commit the error of omission with our colleagues and neglect to share vital information, we have cheated the customer. Every time we take the safe route, staying with the status quo versus using all of our individual and collective talents of boldness and exploration, we have built that wall which will begin closing in on us and will suffocate us in the end.

We are a nation of risk takers, explorers, challengers, and inventors whose strength lies not in the subjugation of the individual nor in group exercises and company songs. As Japan has capitalized on that part of their culture which allows them to meet their business potential, the United States must begin to capitalize on its unique culture and use those elements of high creativity, competition, and desire for personal recognition to drive its businesses. It makes as much sense for us to adopt the Japanese work methods in America as it would to force-fit European work methods in Japan. The shift should be away from adopting and implementing the methodology of the Far East as a panacea for success.

Capitalize On Differences!

The other area of consideration in the yellow brick road is creating the system that best meets the need of your company, its culture, and its customers. This is not accomplished through a canned approach, but by careful design that considers all of the variables that make your company distinct. Part of the idea of superior quality comes from the ability to offer the customer something different, more reliable, faster/easier to use, etc. So for the purpose of improvement and satisfaction, we must not stifle individual differences and creativity but encourage and cultivate them as marketing tools resulting from business successes.

The road to quality for profit can be paved with gold, but it can also be fraught with detours, traffic jams, and head-on collisions. Having the right insurance (knowing the quality road map for success) and thus avoiding danger is critical for successful navigation.

Keeping a united vision for success is crucial to avoid fragmentation. The balance necessary for obtaining a place on the yellow brick road comes from, first knowing where you are and second, understanding where you are headed. Next, determine where you want to be and map out a strategic plan that will lead you through the yellow brick road to your desired destination. For this journey, the following rules of the road will apply:

1. All participants must agree on the destination.

2. No back seat drivers.

3. Wear seat belts for protection.

4. Stay on course.

5. No shortcuts.

When agreeing on the destination, it is mandatory to obtain consensus from those going along for the ride. Direction by dictatorship will not make for a pleasant trip and is a breeder of discontent, resentment, and infighting. Input and agreement on the destination by all parties will alleviate wheel grabbing and general discontent among the passengers. Remember, a smooth ride begins with a good road map and happy passengers. After consensus of the destination has been reached and the passengers are comfortable in their seats, the driver must take the responsibility to ensure a smooth ride for all. Back seat driving is not allowed on the yellow brick road and is a basic sign of lack of trust in the driver. Second guessing the strategic plan and the quality agenda leads to fragmentation and loss of direction.

Buckle Up for Safety

Protection is essential on the yellow brick road and during the execution of the quality plan. Seat belts must be worn at all times and feedback protection is mandatory to stay on track with internal and external customers.

Once on the road, staying on course may include frequent reference to the map, frequent communication with the passengers, and constant focus on traffic, danger signals, and potholes. The challenge is not merely to arrive at the right place at the right time, but to arrive safely with passengers and vehicle intact. It is not enough to have a solid strategic plan and quality improvement plan. To achieve success in customer satisfaction and in the marketplace, *the route* is as important as the goals and the plan. A well-defined route, driven at a comfortable speed in accordance with road conditions and weather factors can mean the difference between ending up safely at your destination or ending up as a hood ornament for a guard rail in the opposite direction.

When discussing the route, a word of caution about shortcuts is appropriate and should be mentioned. A step-by-step, or mile-by-mile approach should be used when executing the quality and customer satisfaction plan. Going too slow can cause a traffic jam and result in an overheated engine. Quality education without quality implementation is like preparing a superior race car for the Indy 500 by admiring it in your garage and taking it out on weekends to drive in traffic at 55 miles per hour. It is the implementation and resultant measurable success that will fuel future successes and bring the corporation closer to the end of the yellow brick road.

In contrast, going too fast will bring about the confusion that comes from running full speed ahead without knowing the plan, the route, or sometimes even the destination. In this case, the act itself becomes the focus of the participants' energies and all else falls by the shoulder of the road. Moving too soon, before all of the facts and data are available, can result in a head-on collision.

In business, like on the road, what you are doing is only half of the story. The other half is keeping track of the competition to anticipate their next move. Reckless driving by the competition can ultimately result in the injury of an innocent party, and that innocent party could be you.

Knowing your competition and what they are likely to do is essential to taking the best position on the road. Misjudgment of the other vehicles could be damaging or fatal, if good pre-test drive data are not available for evaluation before beginning the journey. Some advice for the smart driver: watch front, back, left, and right. Pace yourself at a comfortable cruising speed for the vehicle you are driving and the passengers you are taking for the ride, and at the end of the road success will be within your reach.

● The Pyramid Love Affair— Keeping the Fires Burning

Anthony and Cleopatra, Napoleon and Josephine, Romeo and Juliet—representatives of some of the greatest love affairs of all time. Past or present, fact or fiction, some things will remain the same forever. The elements necessary to develop and sustain a long-lasting personal relationship are the same as those needed for a world class business enterprise. They are fueled by passion, desire, selflessness, and commitment. Sprinkle in a little risk and some compromise and you've got the makings of successful personal and business relationships.

Forming a pyramid of commitment among managers, internal customers, and external customers is much like the pursuit and courtship of a member of the opposite sex. In business, as in love, there are some rules of survival:

Rule Number One: Have a Plan

A plan identifies the goals and criteria by which those goals are to be achieved. In love, it is our concept of the perfect man or woman — all of the physical, intellectual, emotional, and personal data that constitute a perfect match, suitable for living happily ever after. In business, it is the perfect match between the seller and the buyer for products and services that makes for perfect unity.

Rule Number Two: Know Your Competition

In love, knowing the competition is as important as having the secret battle plans of your enemy in war! To win the heart of the object of your affection requires more than simply putting your best foot forward and hoping for the rest to fall into place. Knowing, in detail, about all of the other "feet" that are in hot pursuit of your heart's desire will give you the edge necessary to step on the toes of the competition, thus slowing them down just long enough for you to make your move. In business, the more you know about the competition, the greater your chances of creating a larger market share and of increasing the level of customer service to edge them out. Knowing the internal customer allows for the optimization of teamwork and individual effort necessary for running the ultimate corporate machine. Internally, knowing when to move forward and when to pull back, when to help and when to let things proceed on their own will allow management to maintain perspective and appreciate the contributions of others, and develop potential without the infighting that plagues companies who have not discovered the benefits of organizing for success.

Rule Number Three: Never Resort to Deception

True love is predicated on truth and open lines of communication. Lying, for any reason, is the fastest way to end a beautiful relationship, because it is a by-product of lack of trust, the cornerstone of any relationship worth having. In business, as in private life, how a person deals with colleagues and customers is a reflection of his or her true character. In business, there is no place for lies, half truths, or gray areas. Success will be measured in the 1990s, not in revenues alone, but in the "character" of the business, in contracts fulfilled and in promises kept. World class corporations will not trade revenue for reputation and will not knowingly deceive a customer in favor of a sale nor decline to honor a valid return.

Rule Number Four: Always Remember Passion

In nature and in affairs of the heart, it takes a spark to make a fire. In love, passion is the spark that ignites the eternal flame. It is the element that separates infatuation and relationships of convenience from the true, enduring "real thing." Keeping love alive involves taking the spark of passion and fanning it into a smoldering ember. Essential to keeping passion in a relationship is change, innovation, and an element of surprise.

In business, a passion for work and a passion for serving the customer are essential. Far too often, business people "settle" for something that "pays the bills" but brings them no personal satisfaction. This is work without passion, flat, mechanical, and detached, without form or depth. For these people, work is an eight-hour numbness, endured to support a certain lifestyle. It has nothing to do with a sense of accomplishment and exhilaration that comes from landing a prize contract, solving a customer problem, or designing a new product. If we were to approach our work with the same passion we have for a lover or our favorite sport, we could make mediocre products into superior ones and keep the customer coming back for more.

Rule Number Five: It's Not How You Look, It's What You Are

Part of the reason we have failed to produce superior products and services lies with our approach to our business and with our business' approach to us. In the 1980s, we sold our dreams for a BMW and a key to the executive washroom. In doing so, we lost the vision, drive, and passion of a Henry Ford, a Thomas Edison, and a Walt Disney. We stopped taking risks and shooting for the impossible dream in favor of shooting from the hip, the sure thing, and the quick fix. We settled for the ordinary and the comfortable and turned our backs on the challenges and ideals of our youth.

At the same time that workers were engulfed in a sea of apathy, walking through the mechanics of their jobs. Corporations developed bureaucracies more intricate than government security systems to discourage, frustrate, and baffle the work force. Buried in a barrage of paperwork, endless meetings, reviews, and approvals that sapped creative energy and weakened performance, we stopped worrying about the customer and constantly worried about the budget. There was money for elaborate off-sight meetings and management perks. There were funds to repair and replace poor product quality before shipping and still more money to correct, replace, or recall poor products in the field. There was no money to increase the salaries of high performers, but funds were always available for overtime due to inadequate forecasts, lack of inventory control, mismanagement, and nonconforming materials.

The emphasis was on the trappings and not on the substance of success. The corporation wanted the right school not the right candidate, the right suit not the right mind, and the party line not free thinking. The eighties was a decade when the word "power" referred to ties and lunches, and no longer was used to describe the ability to harness and utilize the strength of the work force to excel in the marketplace.

We anguished more over the proper dress for success attire than we did over serving the customer and the outcome was devastating. While we preened, polished, and perfected ourselves, consumed power lunches and wore power ties, the power shifted to the Far East. Our customers suffered and business declined. We had cut corners, cut communications, and in the end, cut our own throats—all in the name of success. The bottom line was that our love affair had become a love-hate relationship that we have had to rebuild.

The good news is, after all the fads, the gimmicks, and the Japanese hype, we have rediscovered what we should have known all along: The power to realize our dreams in business to persevere against the most difficult odds is in our own backyard.

Rule Number Six: It's OK to Agree to Disagree

Like most partnerships, it is not always smooth sailing. Working together to solve problems in both personal and business relationships sometimes has its moments when one side must suspend the argument and concede to the other side. This can be done in such a way so as not to lose the respect of the other person and maintain the relationship. The focus of discussion aimed at improvement of products and services, or the introduction of new ideas, should not be based on personal victory but on sound business sense and a customer perspective.

Once the approach to decision making and problem solving is depersonalized, agreement, disagreement, and concession can be made without fear of injury to the relationship. Disagreement within the ranks should not be construed as lack of commitment to the department, lack of support for the manager, or mutiny. It represents a healthy exercising of one's right to disagree and express a different opinion. This should not be interpreted as a show of no confidence, but as a tribute to the relationship and to a management style that encourages free thinking without fear of reprisal. This is not to be confused with the infighting, backstabbing, and sabotage discussed in earlier chapters. To have a healthy disagreement in business and be able to move forward with the relationship intact is part of the success story of a quality organization.

Disagreement can be a positive experience by allowing differences to be aired freely and new ideas considered without having them become major breeding grounds for resentment, or weapons to be brought out later and used to embarrass or demean the other person. Remember, in a democracy there are no absolute, imperial rulers!

Rule Number Seven: Show Consideration

Respecting the needs and rights of others is just good manners. It is also good business. Learning to work with others in a way that promotes consideration of each other and of the customer is the key to harmony in the workplace and makes teamwork a pleasant experience. Part of being accepted involves being considerate of the feelings of others. The quickest way to lose a relationship, alienate a team of workers, or anger a customer is to take them for granted. Consideration of others shows caring, respect, and the desire to please. When these elements are present through one's actions, the customer is shown that he or she is valued and that the relationship will be preserved. With our colleagues, keeping them informed of our progress on key issues will show consideration of their positions in the corporate quality process and encourage reciprocal behavior.

In addition to the consideration shown by informing others of progress on vital issues, the inclusion of others by invitation to the processes of brainstorming and problem solving is another way to show people they are valued in the organization.

Rule Number Eight: Be Resourceful

This may be the most difficult of all of the challenges in the pyramid love affair. Over time it becomes more difficult to maintain the early excitement experienced when a product or service was new, a cutting edge technology was introduced, or a major problem resolved. It is at this point when people are tempted to become complacent, that they must resist the temptation to fall into a rut and lose ground. Exercising resourcefulness means realizing there is more than one way to get to the pot of gold at the end of the rainbow and more than one way to reach a solution to a problem.

Motivating people is a full-time job. Exciting them, challenging them, and creating the kind of environment which encourages excellence requires digging for all of the resources you can find and using every one of them. Trying a new method, using a different approach, or inventing a new system are examples of ways in which people can use their imaginations in attaining a higher quality standard.

Rule Number Nine: Never Say Never

A positive attitude and the belief that all things are possible is the inspiration that creates greatness and forms unbreakable relationships.

Perhaps the greatest test of strength and the true meaning of relationships has a lot to do with the obstacles overcome and the difficulties endured to preserve them. It is easy to maintain balance and harmony when things are moving along without major problems. It is when we face tough business decisions about the present and future that will impact ourselves, and those who work for us (and ultimately the customer) that never saying never is most important. To give up without a fight is the mark of a loser. There is the famous story of Fred Smith, founder of Federal Express, who early in his college career developed the notion of a mail service that could move mail from one place to another, anywhere in the world . . . *overnight!* Smith used this radical theory as the basis for a college project and was not only given a below average grade on the paper, but the indignity of a caption written by his professor saying that the idea was ridiculous!

Undaunted, Smith pursued his dreams to achieve fame and fortune. The journey over Smith's yellow brick road was not a smooth ride. Plagued by money problems, the story goes that Smith gambled the last $100 of the business' money in hope of making the company solvent. In the true style of a risk taker and in the face of what would seem impossible to many, Smith risked everything, never said never, and *won!*

Everyone knows the ending of this story. Smith went on to become successful beyond maybe even his own dreams. Federal Express enjoys the prestige of being a superior company at fulfilling the customers' needs. And the professor? He's probably writing obituaries for a local paper. What's that saying? "Those that can, do; those that can't, teach!"

In business, it is a never say never attitude that will enable impossible situations to have a real chance for resolution. It is the ultimate test of one's ability to beat the odds, come from behind, and cross the finish line first. To pull it off, we must have the confidence and trust in ourselves and in each other that lets us believe that the impossible is truly possible and that only the obstacles of our own invention stand in the way of success. Our fear of failure, the unknown, reprisal, and rejection paralyze our abilities to question, formulate a plan, and find an answer.

In the final analysis, when all is said and done, it is the people who make up the organization and the customers they pledge to serve who will have the greatest impact on whether or not business will succeed. Whether the organization uses a scientific quality approach or rejects it, whether the organization listens to the needs of customers or turns a deaf ear, whether it believes that the power to advance and achieve greatness rests with each individual in the organization or lies in technology alone, will determine the corporate destiny.

Bibliography

Clausing, Donald. "The House of Quality." *Harvard Business Review*, January 1988: 24.

Crosby, Philip B. *Quality Is Free.* New York: McGraw-Hill Book Co., 1979.

Harrington, H. James. *Poor-Quality Cost.* Milwaukee: ASQC Quality Press, 1987.

Imai, Masaaki. *Kaizen The Key to Japan's Competitive Success.* New York: Random House, 1968.

Juran, Joseph M., and Frank M. Gryna, Jr. *Quality Planning and Analysis.* New York: McGraw-Hill Book Co., 1980.

Westland, Cynthia L. "Avoid the Just-in-Time Terrors." *Quality Progress* 21, No. 10 (October 1988): 69-70.

Index

Endurance, 3
   companies of, 3
Euphoria, Twinkie defense for the artificial, 73-74
External costs, 13

F

Federal Express, 105
Feedback, 19, 35-36
Flexibility, 3
Flexible companies, 3
Freedom of Information Act, 49

G

Gimmicks, 55

H

Harrington, H. James, 96
Head in the sand approach, 63
Health care setting, quality cost assessment in, 17
Hearing loss, 21
Hirsutism, 23
House on shifting sand theory, 27-28
Hydrocephalus, 22
Hyperactivity, 23
Hypoglycemia, 22

I

IDM. *See* Improvement dynamics management
   (IDM)
"I'm OK, you're not" syndrome, 7
Implementation suicide, 29
Improvement dynamics management, 34-43

Management by intimidation technique, 85-87
Managerial losers
    Ivan the terrible, 85-87
    juggler, 80-82
    Mr. Happy Face, 82-83
    Mr. Potato Head, 84-85
    recluse, 78-80
Managerial overload, 80-82
Manic depression, 25
Marketing strategy, quality as a, 44-46
Masochism, 25
Middle management. *See* Quality cost analysis
Migraine, 22
Minute waltz, 61-62
Mobile customer satisfaction units, 57, 91-92
Monday morning quarterback, value of, 63-66
Motivation, of people, 104-105
Mr. Happy Face, as managerial loser, 82-83
Mr. Potato Head, as managerial loser, 84-85
Mushroom's disease, 23

N

Names/phrases, recognition of key, 20
Narcissistic personality, 24
Needs identification, use of, in customer satisfaction, 89-96
Never say never attitude, 105-106

O

Obsessive-compulsive, 24
100 percent inspection, 84
Optimism, in management, 82-83

P

Panacea of the month club, 28
Paranoia, 71-73, 86-87

W

Weave and dodge technique, 79
Win-win situations, 59-60
Wolfman's Wisp Disease, 23
Women, in the workplace, 90
Work ethic, quality-by-example versus
    quality-by-exception, 7
Work flow analysis, 37
    use of, in improvement dynamics management, 37-38
Work force
    reduction of, and quality improvement, 29
    responsibility of, for customer satisfaction, 54
    signs of disturbed, 21-22

Y

"Yuppies," 90